FLEXIBILITY FOR MARTIAL ARTS AND FITNESS

YOUR ULTIMATE STRETCHING AND WARM-UP GUIDE!

Unlock your body's potential...

PHIL PIERCE

All content Copyright © 2020

WHAT CAN YOU GET FROM THIS BOOK?

- **Do you know the shocking research changing everything we know about flexibility?**
- Or why stretching doesn't work ... the way you think?!
- **Discover the exact stretches required for faster, stronger punches and kicks**
- And greater range for all of your strikes
- **Exposed: The most common killer mistake and which stretches are actually reducing your strength!**
- Learn the fool-proof exercise that is more effective than 90% of so-called 'warm-ups'
- **The _____ method for looser muscles**
- How to push your limits and stay safe
- **The 3 forms of stretching (and why you might already be more flexible than you know)**
- How to banish the causes of inflexibility
- **How to speed up your muscle recovery**
- *And much more!*

The simple aim of this book is to unlock your body's potential and show you the powerful and effective stretches, mobility exercises and warm-ups that take your flexibility to the next level! (And reveal the surprising mistakes you may already be making.)

With the latest research from top sports coaches, martial artists and trainers, the techniques and methods within this guide are all designed to be easy to follow, simple to perform and allow you to really maximize your training regime through improved suppleness, greater range-of-motion and reduced risk of injury.

Whether you are a martial arts student, an MMA fighter or just a fitness fan, discover how to unlock your flexibility today...

CONTENTS

Flexibility For Martial Arts and Fitness	1
What Can You Get From This Book?	3
Prefer to Watch as you Learn?	9
How You Can Perform Stronger and Faster Through Flexibility	11
Getting the Best 'Bang-For-Buck' From Your Stretching	13

PART ONE
THE SCIENCE OF STRETCHING SIMPLIFIED

What is Flexibility? (And why should I bother?)	19
Forms of Flexibility	23
Why am I So Inflexible Right Now?	27
Stretching Doesn't Work ... The Way You Think	31
The Flexibility Myth (The Science of Stretching)	35
Myotatic Reflex – Nature's Flexibility Barrier	39
Golgi Tendon Reflex - Your Ally in Stretching	41
The Power of Isometric Stretching	45
Forms of Stretching	51
Ballistic Stretches	55
Dynamic Stretches	57
Proprioceptive Neuromuscular Facilitation (PNF)	61

PART TWO
IMPROVING YOUR STRETCHING SUCCESS

When do I Stretch as Part of My Training?	65
How Often Should I Stretch?	69
The Most Common Stretching Mistake	73
The 'Rocking' Trick for Faster Flexibility	77
Stretching Mistake 2: No Pain No Gain	81
Understanding the Pain Scale	83
Faster Muscle Recovery	89

Why You Should Be Stretching Opposing Muscle Groups	93
Working with a Partner vs. Going it Alone	99

PART THREE
WARM-UPS MADE EASY

Stretching vs. Warming Up: Why You Need To Know The Difference	105
Foolproof Warm-Ups using SAID	111

PART FOUR
DYNAMIC MOBILITY

How to Extend the Reach of Your Strikes and Blocks	117
How to Perform Dynamic Mobility Circles	121
Don't Forget to Work Your Wrists and Ankles (Why and How)	125
Ankle Mobility Exercises	127
Wrist Mobility Exercises	131

PART FIVE
THE STRETCHES

Starting the Stretches	137
WARM-UPS	139
JOINT ROTATIONS	145
DYNAMIC STRETCHES	153
STATIC AND ISOMETRIC STRETCHES	169
How to Stretch the Full Body (Routines)	199

PART SIX
TAKING IT FURTHER

How to Make Stretching a Regular Habit	205
Crafting Your Stretching Routine	213
Test Your Progress with Measured Kicks	217
The 'Trick' to Long-Term Flexibility	221
Cheat Sheet: Your Stretching Simplified	225

Thank You For Reading	229
Ready for More Flexibility?	231

PREFER TO WATCH AS YOU LEARN?

Books are great, but they aren't for everyone. If you prefer to watch and follow along as you learn, discover **How to Stretch for Martial Arts, MMA and Self Defense: Your Ultimate Stretching and Warm up Guide** ... the video course!

https://geni.us/flexibility

What's inside?

- Over 80 videos, packed with proven stretches and techniques to increase flexibility.
- Step-by-step guide through safe and effective warm-ups.
- Dynamic stretches for increased range of motion and mobility.
- The exact methods for releasing muscle tension for faster, higher kicks, and longer-reaching strikes.
- Stretching 'hacks' so you can cheat your way to increased flexibility quicker than ever.
- And more!

Visit: **https://geni.us/flexibility** and unlock the potential in your flexibility today!

HOW YOU CAN PERFORM STRONGER AND FASTER THROUGH FLEXIBILITY

Welcome to Flexibility for Martial Arts, MMA, and Fitness. Your Ultimate Stretching and Warm-Up Guide.

Whether you are training in a specific martial art, competing against others, or you just want to develop increased flexibility and a rock-solid warm-up routine for your fitness goals, this book can help you unlock the potential of your body, through powerful, step-by-step methods that anyone can follow.

The techniques and stretches contained within this book have been collected from a variety of expert sources, including top performance coaches, martial arts instructors and a variety of sports trainers with proven results. All designed to give you the edge in your training.

The first part of this book will explore why and how stretching works (Clue: it's probably not what you think), the science behind stretching and more importantly, how we can use this surprising information to our advantage.

In the second part, we have a series of proven tactics for improving your stretching success, including techniques for preventing injury for life, how to increase your results faster and the mindset for stretching success.

Parts three and four get into some physical techniques with warm-ups and mobility exercises. Simple, effective movements you can perform to prepare the body for action and increase your range of motion and reach.

In the final section, part five, we get into the actual stretches, with a series of flexibility-increasing exercises for all ability levels, starting with the upper body and working through the head and neck, chest, back, arms, hips, and legs. All to develop faster, higher strikes and greater ease of movement for your training.

So, if you're ready to unlock the potential in your body, let's go!

GETTING THE BEST 'BANG-FOR-BUCK' FROM YOUR STRETCHING

Author's Note:

Over the years, I have been lucky enough to experience a great number of training methods all across the world. I've written a couple of bestsellers within the fitness and martial arts genres and I've learned from some of the best coaches and instructors around. One of the enduring lessons I've learned is that everyone, regardless of ability, can improve. Whatever your current level, you can get better and, given the right methods, reach your flexibility goals.

But it's not always easy if you go it alone. After all, in the modern age, information overload is very real. Thousands of experts, offer hundreds of techniques across videos, books, and forums for every subject imaginable. All *might* have value, but how do you know where to begin?

With this book, I aim to make things more simple, using something called the Pareto Principle.

If you've never heard of the Pareto principle, it's a subject worth reading up on a little. When I was younger I discovered this concept and it became somewhat of a guiding light in my life, my training, and my flexibility practices. As such, it also underpins this guide.

Sometimes called the 80/20 rule or the Law of Vital Few, it essentially states that for most things in life, 80% of our returns come from 20% of our efforts. In other words, many of the actions we undertake in life are at best, giving us minimal returns, and at worst, not doing anything at all. Conversely, a small number of the actions we perform regularly, are actually the things that affect our lives the most.

The first time I heard this concept I was surprised. Could it really be true that many of the actions we take in life are simply wasting time and producing minimal results?

Turns out, yes.

In fact, studies have shown that in sports and exercise, in particular, roughly 20% of the exercises and habits we perform, have 80% of the impact on our ultimate performance, essentially implying that a hugely complex training regime is a waste of time.

After looking at my own training, looking at the work I do and in particular, the flexibility training I undertook, it became clear that while I was often working hard, only a small number of the exercises and stretches I performed were actually making any noticeable difference and the same can be true for you.

This concept behind the Pareto Principle also underpins much of this book and the stretches included within. The truth is that there are hundreds, if not thousands of stretches an individual can practice to improve flexibility through the body. An overwhelming wealth of information and exercises exist out there, but the problem is that many of these drills offer minimal benefit to the average person and the time taken to learn then diminishes any return you may get.

Take dancers for example. There exists a widely practiced series of stretches for developing the splits. A powerful, proven sequence of passive and active stretches and drills. Unfortunately, the sequence involves over thirty different techniques and takes almost two hours to complete. Every day. Fine if you are a professional dancer, training full-time, but for most of us, we want simple effective stretches we can do in a few minutes, not a few hours.

Which is where this book comes in. The exercises and practices included are designed to give you the best 'bang for buck' in terms of time spent and energy used, and ultimately offer the best returns (improvements in flexibility) for your efforts.

If you are looking for a specific stretch and it's not listed here, that's not to say it isn't effective, or that it's not a good stretch. It's simply the case that for this book, choices had to be made about which stretches to include and which to omit. Giving you the best 'bang-for-buck' is a priority.

If you are interested in taking your flexibility work further, look out for my future books and videos on the subject, where I will be exploring more advanced techniques, but for now, these are the stretches which I, and many others, have found to offer the most benefit.

I hope you find it useful!

Phil Pierce

PART ONE
THE SCIENCE OF STRETCHING SIMPLIFIED

WHAT IS FLEXIBILITY? (AND WHY SHOULD I BOTHER?)

Simply put, flexibility is: "Moving your body through its best potential range of movement."

Also known as being limber, flexibility is the range of movement of a joint or multiple joints and the associated length of muscle fibers working across and around that joint, to achieve bending or motion.

Muscle tissue, for example, is typically arranged in bundled parallel fibers and is comprised of stretchy material that moves easily.

Similarly, some connective tissues employ yellow elastic tissue which is open to considerable stretching. These types of fibers, respond well to a flexibility program and it's within these parts of the body you will see the benefits.

On, the other hand, ligaments, and tendons also use white fibrous tissue; the tissue which keeps things in place, and this while very strong, is not flexible at all.

Some tissues of the body are far more easily stretchable than others, but that doesn't matter as much as you might think (we'll explore why soon), but overall, flexibility is something that can easily be improved over time by training and conditioning.

Why should I bother?

Unfortunately, most people give little thought to flexibility training. Let's face it, when you are short on time or energy, stretching and flexibility work might seem like the most logical activity to skip. From outside appearances, stretching won't help you lose weight, get stronger, or give you the chiseled abs you've seen on TV.

It's true that you'll see more of a physical difference and probably garner more compliments by engaging in cardio or strength training.

Which of course raises the question…why should I bother?

The first thing to understand is that flexibility is actually just as important as things like strength and endurance training, especially so in the case of the martial artist or fitness fan.

With flexibility comes better posture, and while you may not look much different from the outside, you can feel decades younger when you start to move in a more natural, unimpeded way.

Speaking of which, perhaps the best advantage of flexibility is being able to move with fluidity and ease through your full potential. If you've ever marveled at how a conditioned Shaolin monk is able to perform with such grace and strength, how a dancer flows between positions, or how top athletes and fighters make techniques look effortless, the answer is undoubtedly increased flexibility.

Some people might define flexibility as the ability to touch their toes, but it really is so much more than that. Being flexible is being able to move freely in your own body.

There's a lot of confidence to be found in moving without pain or discomfort, and also from being able to assume the most complex postures perfectly and without tension. When you develop good flexibility, every action you take will put less stress and strain on your body, which means you'll be able to do a lot more. You'll be able to train harder and recover more quickly than ever before.

It's not just anecdotal evidence either. Thousands of studies demonstrate the benefits of improved flexibility.

Harvard health, for example, confirmed in a 2019 study that real flexibility also has the ability to improve your balance, something every martial artist strives to maintain. Balance is the ability to distribute your weight appropriately to remain upright. This is easy when standing still, but takes on a greater challenge when difficult postures or external forces come into play; especially things like high kicks and jumping techniques. Flexible muscles and ligaments are able to fine-tune your stance without being thrown off. That means you'll have better luck standing your ground when an opponent lunges in your direction or an obstacle appears out of thin air.

Flexibility is also extra valuable when taking part in any activity that places additional stress on the joints and muscles like kicking and punching. For instance, if you have performed a few side-kicks then you may have observed the way your lower back and outer hip naturally become tighter. If you were to continuously perform this movement without stretching, then you'll likely begin to experience some back pain. Not only is this pain unpleasant but it also will, unfortunately, limit your ability to improve your performance. Back pain is common in martial arts, but it doesn't have to be.

Stretching allows you to open this area so you can keep kicking. Not only that, but you'll be able to kick higher and with less resistance, ultimately using less energy to make the technique. This conservation of energy means you are less exhausted and can go longer than an opponent, giving you a better chance in sparring or competitive environments.

It might not seem like it, but staying flexible really does give you an edge in almost every sport. Side-kicks are just one example too. Real flexibility can enhance every aspect of your training, whether you are a martial artist, MMA fighter, runner, dancer or weekend athlete.

As a bonus, stretching also helps to flush the toxins that can build up in muscles during physical exertion. As you train, your body is put under stress, causing substances like lactic acid to build up in your muscles (Juel, 2004). You are probably familiar with the unpleasant lactic acid burning sensation and the longer-lasting muscle soreness. Dynamic stretching after your training session is proven to be one of the most powerful tools when it comes to flushing lactic acid from your muscles. In addition to helping you avoid discomfort, you'll also experience reduced inflammation and faster muscle recovery time—a good reason to take a few minutes to stretch after every training session.

If none of that appeals to you then consider that a more flexible muscle at rest will contract faster and with greater force when in use, allowing you to use the maximum amount of power. That means faster and stronger kicks and punches.

Improving your flexibility is a scientifically proven method for improving both your athletic performance and your quality of life as a whole.

FORMS OF FLEXIBILITY

When you think of flexibility, you may just think of how much a person can bend in any given direction but in fact, there are three main forms of flexibility and these are especially applicable to students practicing combat arts. You may even be surprised to learn that the ability to do the splits, for example, doesn't necessarily mean you are flexible in all forms. Indeed, you may already be more flexible than you think in some forms, while less-so in others.

In the following chapter, we will take a look at the three flexibility forms and learn how flexibility in one form doesn't always mean flexibility in another.

1. **Dynamic Flexibility.**

This is perhaps the most useful form of flexibility especially if you are practicing martial arts like Karate, Taekwondo or other traditional styles. That said, it also helps MMA fighters and anyone requiring occasional high kicks and strikes.

Dynamic flexibility is all about using energy and motion. In other words, it is flexibility through movement. Dynamic techniques work by engaging the major agonist (active) muscle and relaxing the antagonist or opposite muscle. These muscles are often paired in sets called a flexor and extensor. The flexor being the muscle contracting and the extensor relaxing.

In dynamic flexibility, you make a technique through the full range of motion, engaging the joints, connective tissues, and muscle fibers as it extends fully. A simple example of this would be a straight-leg forward leg swing.

An interesting aspect of dynamic flexibility is that you can maximize your dynamic ability and develop very high and very powerful kicks, without maximizing your static flexibility. This means that your ability to do (or not do) the splits does not affect your ability to throw out killer kicks. This fact alone is a great reason to put dynamic training high on your list.

It's also the easiest form of flexibility to improve for most people.

2. Static Flexibility

Sometimes also called static-passive flexibility or simply 'reach' flexibility, this is the most famous form of flexibility, demonstrated through engaging your maximum reach or bend and holding the position. It's an old-school method of measuring your movement and has been around for a long time, but still has value today.

Still confused? Just think of the splits. This is a classic form of static flexibility since the practitioner is moving into and holding a single position at the end of the movement. It's a form that does have value within the martial arts community but not as often as dynamic movements.

Still, static flexibility seems to be the one people are most obsessed with and keen to improve. If that's you, there are actually a few different methods for doing this, including static stretches (no surprise) and Isometric or Muscle Energy Stretches—which are typically more effective. All of these will be explored later.

Static flexibility sits in the middle ground in terms of difficulty.

3. Active Flexibility

If you've ever spent any time online watching martial arts demonstrations, or cast an eye over action movies from the '80s and '90s, it's likely you've seen those amazing demonstrations of limb control, where the hero or star of the video, picks a leg up and slowly kicks it vertical only to hold it there in an incredible display of strength and balance.

This is active flexibility, where the practitioner is making a technique and holding it using muscle strength, in particular, that of the primary agonist muscle, giving the antagonist muscle a stretch.

If you wanted to throw a high kick and hold it, for example, you might engage the quadriceps (agonists) and the hamstrings become the antagonists. The kick is held through the power of the quads and give the hamstrings a stretch.

The interesting thing is that while these kicks and stretches look amazing, they don't have much value in martial arts or combat sports. It's quite rare to need to hold a high kick for long and unless you are training for specific gymnastic or demonstration purposes you won't find much mileage in them.

Active flexibility is also the hardest form of flexibility to master.

WHY AM I SO INFLEXIBLE RIGHT NOW?

Are you stiff as a board and wondering why?

Over my many years as a martial arts and fitness coach, there have been a hundred and one reasons given for an individual's flexibility – or lack of. Usually a mixture of the truth, a sprinkle of pseudo-science and some far-fetched excuse. Some people blame the weather, others blame diet, while some still believe its fate or some divine intervention affecting their range of motion.

Actually, it's far more simple.

Simply put, research has shown that natural flexibility is determined by a combination of the three things;

- **Physical build, (and genes)**
  - If both of your parents were Olympic gymnasts you have a good chance at inheriting some of this natural muscular ability.
- **Age**
  - Perhaps not surprisingly, age is a big factor.
- **The overall health of your body and specifically ligaments, tendons, and muscles.**
  - If you smoke fifty a day and have a poor diet expect this to be reflected in your flexibility.

As we get older and, ultimately less active, our flexibility reduces naturally, as our body and the nervous system adapts to a more sedentary lifestyle. Through this, muscles and connective tissues become tight through disuse. Think of a car engine. Unused for weeks on end it seizes up and becomes harder to start.

Unfortunately, we live in an age where huge percentages of people work in an office or computer-based environment. This lifestyle, often combined with little exercise in our free time, leads to long term deterioration of our health and flexibility.

The good news is that the reverse is also true. Your body adapts to its surroundings and the challenges placed on it. With the introduction of a little stretching and exercise, you can 'teach' your body to improve.

This is why a little exercise and stretching can be some of the most important things you can do for your long-term health. A short but regular exercise regime that includes flexibility training can help to prevent or at least slow down the stiffness via the aging process and improve overall well-being.

Women (may) have a head start.

One interesting aspect of flexibility is that while men typically have a lower body fat and higher muscle density at a genetic level, giving them advantages in the strength stakes, women usually win out in the flexibility game.

At an anatomical level, females generally have greater hip movement and flexibility, due to different bone structure. Studies also show they feature much higher levels of a hormone called Relaxin, produced in the ovaries. This chemical, a crucial part of childbirth, is present in all women, pregnant or otherwise, and relaxes the connective tissues around the pelvis allowing for a greater range of motion.

The Splits Myth

If there exists one technique that fascinates and terrifies in equal measure, it's the splits. Most people would love to perform it, and many try and fail, with varying levels of pain. The interesting thing about the splits is that as a technique, it's not very useful nor is it needed to perform high kicks.

Sure, it looks good and might impress your friends at a party, but performing a front or side splits requires a very different kind of flexibility; a static ability over all others. Yes, being good at the splits may give you a very small advantage in other areas, but most martial artists can execute high kicks after a little training without much trouble, despite not achieving the splits. This is due to the fact that kicks normally require dynamic flexibility, not the static variety.

This guide is centered around delivering something I like to call 'functional flexibility. Functional flexibility is all about techniques that deliver results based on the end goal of kicking higher, striking faster and improving your training whatever your sport. Not just for demonstration purposes.

Many of the stretches explored later will help you on the route to achieving the splits if that's your aim, but this isn't the main goal of the book.

As such, don't get hung up on it if you currently feel nowhere near achieving the splits. They are a nice technique to master, but will likely affect your training much less than you think.

STRETCHING DOESN'T WORK ... THE WAY YOU THINK

Stretching isn't what you think it is.

It is a common misconception that the main reason your flexibility increases when you stretch is that your muscles elongate, or become longer. Surprisingly, modern research tells us that this isn't actually true. Stretching will not make your muscles permanently longer because muscle tissues, for example, are attached at fixed points to the bone. They can't really move. The operative word here is the term "permanent", however. As you stretch, the associated muscles do elongate—momentarily—but they don't stay that way.

It is actually important for your muscles to maintain their shape in order to preserve their strength and position. If your muscles actually became stretched out permanently, they would lose their elasticity and strength and our bodies would start to resemble a jellyfish. The complex interplay between tendons, bones, and muscle elasticity is what grants your body strength and mobility. This elasticity is definitely something you want to maintain. It shouldn't be surprising then that a 2014 study measured no significant difference in muscle or tendon length after participants engaged in six weeks of static-stretching (Konrad, 2014), despite an increase in range of motion.

Nonetheless, decades of research and personal experience tell us that stretching does increase long term flexibility. For example, a 2015 study confirmed that both static and modified hold-relax stretching (PNF/Isometric) are effective at increasing hamstring muscle flexibility (Ahmed, 2015). Though, interestingly, the difference between the two wasn't significant enough to determine which was more effective, both forms of stretching improved flexibility compared to the non-stretching control group. Similarly, a Brazilian study in 2011 also measured increased hamstring and hip flexor flexibility after participants engaged in an 8-week flexibility training program (Gallon).

Countless others have also determined that stretching does improve flexibility.

So medically and on an anatomical level, muscles can't be permanently lengthened, but countless studies demonstrate that specific flexibility training does, in fact, seem to work.

The question then is, what's going on here? And by what mechanism does this improvement occur?

Here's another puzzler. Did you know that patients under general anesthetic typically have a complete and full range of motion, with no muscle inhibition? Doctors and surgeons can and do on occasion, swing legs or arms out wide to access the areas they need to operate on, and they get no resistance from the body.

Simply put, if you were knocked out, you could do the splits right now. Which is quite the thought.

While scientists are always working to figure out more about the exact mechanism by which stretching enhances flexibility, studies have shown that we aren't actively increasing muscle or tissue length. It turns out that we are actually stretching our brain and the neurological interpretation of where our 'safe' zones are.

So is flexibility in the mind or in the muscle?

In the next chapter, we will explore exactly this, and how we can use the latest scientific understanding of flexibility to our advantage.

THE FLEXIBILITY MYTH (THE SCIENCE OF STRETCHING)

Let's get technical for a moment and talk about muscles, joints, tendons and ligaments and how their interactions affect your overall flexibility.

Muscles typically consist of fibers (or cells) aligned in a parallel fashion, just like a bundle of wires or cords that might carry the phone or internet line to your house. Studies show that these parallel fibers can contract to approximately 70% of their length compared to resting, and more importantly, can stretch up to 130% longer than resting length. That's a 30% variance in contraction and expansion, you can make use of.

While that might not sound like much, in anatomy terms, it's pretty incredible. What it means is that despite the commonly held belief that some people simply have muscles that are too short to significantly stretch, the science shows that just isn't true. In other words, your muscles don't need any more stretching to increase length. They can already give you a full range of motion right now and every muscle contains amazing potential to be unlocked.

Another way of looking at it is that stretching is not in fact used to elongate muscles and give them longer fibers, that would simply be impossible. Instead, we stretch to condition muscles to accept the stretched position more easily and reduce tension while doing so.

Tendons and Connective Tissue

A connective tissue called Epimysium covers most muscle fibers in the body in a wrap like substance and at the end of each muscle, connects the tissues to the bones surrounding it. This Epimysium or connective tissue hardens as it gets closer and ultimately connects to the bone. At this point, it becomes a 'Tendon'.

Tendons and connective tissues serve several purposes, but one of the main jobs they carry is to be strong, hard and keep the body connected through its series of bones and muscles. Unfortunately, while Tendons are tough and strong, they have low elasticity.

Later in this book, we will discuss something called the Pain Scale. This scale is very important in protecting tendons and connective tissue. While muscles may be able to stretch to 130%, Tendons are unlikely to be anywhere near that flexible. Pushing yourself beyond the pain barrier and forcing your body into a hard stretch (especially without a warm-up) is not only dangerous but can cause long term damage and take you out of action for months.

The good news is that to perform a high kick or even do the splits, you don't need to stretch your tendons, ligaments or joints. In fact, your muscles and tissues are already bendy enough for you to do the splits right now ... even if they don't feel it.

It may be hard to believe, but it's true. At a physiological level, you are already flexible enough to do the splits.

There is no need to increase connective tissue flexibility and no need to lengthen muscles. Your body already has all the range of motion it needs. So if that's true, why can't you drop into the splits right now? Why can't you perform that vertical kick or back-bend?

Here's where things get really interesting. The key to real flexibility is not, in fact, at the muscle level, or the joints. It's in your head. Or more specifically your nervous system and the way it interprets signals from your body.

The secret lies in the reaction your nervous system activates every time you push your muscles beyond its normal range. This signal is what prevents your limbs from relaxing and stops your muscles stretching further. If we can reduce this tightness or tension at a neuromuscular level, we can explore a fuller range of flexibility.

In other words, we need to retrain our body into developing a new reflex during stretches; one that helps us stretch further. But, in fact, there is not just one reflex at work. Anytime you push yourself into a deeper stretch, two reflexes are battling it out for domination.

MYOTATIC REFLEX – NATURE'S FLEXIBILITY BARRIER

Your whole body is constantly controlled at a subconscious level by your brain and the neurological signals it receives from sensors in every part of your being. These signals are flying around all the time, regulating everything from digestion and sleep, to movement and even breathing.

The length and movement of your muscles are no exception. The muscle fibers control the muscular tension and this, in turn, is controlled by signals firing back and forth through your nervous system.

When you perform a stretch beyond your usual range of motion, sensors within tissue called Muscle Spindles start to fire. These Spindles are string-like sensors, which can react to the length of the stretch, the speed of the stretch of both. They send warning signals to your neuromuscular system, through the spinal cord up to the brain. The brain then sends a signal to tighten the muscle and increase tension, to keep you safe or keep you balanced.

This reflex is in effect in every muscle within your body. When you make an abrupt or exaggerated movement, the reflex acts as a resistance, limiting the movement within the muscle. You have likely observed this in the tension felt through a stretch or high kick. Moving beyond that point of resistance causes your nervous system to send pain signals to your brain. Like any reflex, it can be both a blessing and a curse. Some athletes, find it a hindrance in the way it can sometimes limit their training abilities but it also ensures that progress is found gradually and therefore more safely.

An in-built injury prevention system.

Each time your muscle is moved in an extreme or unfamiliar way, it almost instantaneously gets a signal to contract and tightens up to protect itself.

This actually serves several purposes at an evolutionary level:

- Prevents muscle tears and damage
- Prevents falling
- Prevents becoming unbalanced
- Keeps you able to defend yourself from danger

This important reflex is known as the Myotatic Reflex, Stretch Reflex or Reciprocal Inhibition. All of which are quite a mouthful, so for the purposes of this guide we will simply refer to it as the Myotatic Reflex. This Myotatic Reflex is actually what is holding you back from achieving your full potential flexibility, not your muscles. It's this reflex that tells the muscle to 'hold up', 'slow down' and 'tighten up'. It's also the biggest obstacle we must overcome to fully unlock flexibility.

Luckily, the Myotatic Reflex has a twin, and this one helps us out much more.

GOLGI TENDON REFLEX - YOUR ALLY IN STRETCHING

Have you ever exercised so hard that you got to a point where you simply couldn't work anymore and slumped on the floor? This is the principle of the Golgi Tendon Reflex and it's one we want to encourage.

Golgi Tendon Organs (GTOs) are a similar, but different kind of stretch receptor to the Muscle Spindles we mentioned a moment ago. These receptors measure the amount of force developed by a muscle and changes in muscle tension. They are also crucial in developing a relaxation response for increased flexibility.

When these GTOs sense too much overwhelming force applying to muscle tissue and/or tendon tissue in a static position, they send a signal through the neuromuscular system, telling the brain to let the muscle 'relax'. This reflex is known as the Golgi Tendon Reflex (GTR) or Autogenic Inhibition Reflex and it can be your greatest ally in stretching.

The Golgi Tendon Reflex is the sudden 'giving up' or relaxation of a muscle in response to excess tension. The signal fires through the nervous system and is regulated by specific proprioceptors or sensors in the tendons near the muscle, largely controlled by the GTOs we just mentioned.

How does it work?

Like its twin, the Golgi Tendon Reflex is actually a survival mechanism. A safety feature built into our bodies. While the Myotatic reflex is important to keep us upright and kicking, there comes a point where the body senses the stress and tension is simply too much for the Myotatic Reflex to handle and the GTR takes over.

At this point, the GTR switches off the muscle tension because the nervous system is telling the body that to continue resisting will cause tearing or permanent muscle damage.

So how can we use this to our advantage?

Sure, we want to avoid injury and muscle damage is no fun, but what if we could trick the body into engaging that relaxation reflex, without the risk of injury? Then we would have a secret weapon in increasing flexibility.

We know that when we stretch normally into our maximum range, the Myotatic Reflex quickly kicks in holding us back. It tightens the muscle to prevent further stretch. Typically, about seven to ten seconds later, the Golgi Tendon Reflex starts to engage, relaxing the muscle slightly. This happens when the body senses no immediate danger and realizes that relaxing the muscle is preferable. This can then be repeated three or four times to maximize the training of our Golgi Tendon Reflex and 'teach' the body it is ok to move this way.

This is the fundamental principle of how traditional stretching works and how it increases flexibility. In fact, it's how all the stretches in this book, and any other book, works.

But ... there exists one problem with this method ... it's typically ... very ... slow.

In the next chapter, we will look at a higher-risk, higher reward approach to stretching, that offers much faster results.

THE POWER OF ISOMETRIC STRETCHING

You can hammer away for years following the basic stretching process, all the while trying to increase the body's tolerance for stretching and gradually teaching the nervous system, Myotatic Reflex, and Golgi Tendon Reflex to accept your new ways of moving the muscle tissue.

It's safe, it's effective and very slow.

It's a method most martial arts schools use, and I'll be honest, it works, but at such a gradual level that most students get frustrated with a lack of progress and either quit stretching or give up the training altogether!

In this chapter, I want to show you a secret weapon for enhancing our stretches and a method by which you can see actual physical improvements in flexibility over minutes, not years.

It has several names including PNF and Muscle Energy Technique, but for simplicity, we are going to use the popular term; Isometric Stretching, and I believe it's one of the most powerful stretching tools available.

Originally developed by doctors to aid stroke victims and then adopted by physiotherapists and body-workers to help athletes in recovery, these techniques were created to engage a practitioner's body and use their own energy to help them heal and overcome injury. The real magic started happening when a small number of coaches and fitness fans started realizing the potential for the techniques in quickly enhancing flexibility.

We know that the Myotatic Reflex starts after a stretch to protect the body and after a time of approximately seven seconds (up to thirty) the Golgi Tendon Reflex takes over relaxing the muscle and allowing a further stretch. But how much further?

Usually not much at all. A few millimeters maybe? Half an inch if you are lucky.

The Golgi Reflexive relaxation is directly related to the tension and stresses the muscle experiences, and since a gentle stretch rarely triggers much in the way of this tension, only a small number of muscle fibers actually end up relaxing, while the majority stay tight and tense. Which is why even regular stretching often yields slow results.

But what if we could trick the muscle into thinking it was under greater stress?

If we could trigger a greater response from more of the muscle fibers and in turn, more of the GTOs, we could get a greater relaxation response and a bigger overall 'letting go' of the muscle, leading to increased flexibility.

This is where Isometric Stretching comes in.

If for any given stretch, you consciously tense (contract) the stretched muscle before you drop into the next part of the stretch, you involve greater muscle fibers and more of these get activated and ultimately relaxed through the Golgi Tendon Reflex, leading to stretching further. Typically beyond what you could achieve beforehand.

In other words, the **tense-stretch-relax** process enables us to stretch beyond our normal maximum range of flexibility. Repeat this process three to four times for optimal benefit and suddenly we are increasing how far we can bend in measurable centimeters or inches in *each session*, not over years!

How to do Isometric Stretches:

This method is applicable to almost any stretch because the process works the same regardless of the muscle involved. Remember, however, that a warm-up and proper mobility exercises first are always essential, especially in high intensity stretching such as this. See the chapter entitled 'When do I stretch," for more details on when/where to incorporate Isometrics into your routine.

For this example, we will use a straight leg, hamstring and calf stretch.

1. After a warm-up, and while standing, slowly kick one leg out straight and place it on a chair/sofa/table/whatever. Place it at a height where you feel the stretch, but not any pain.
2. Take your baseline measurement, by leaning forward and reaching with your hands toward your toes of the straight leg. Keep those toes pointing skyward.
3. Reach the toes? Great. If not, just reach for the ankle or shin, whatever works for you. This point is only about getting a rough measure of your current level – don't overdo it.
4. Relax and come back up to standing.
5. This time using about 30% of your power, kick down with the outstretched leg into the chair for approx. 5 seconds. (Make sure the chair is stable and won't suddenly move!)
6. Relax the muscles and reach down to the toes once more, possibly going a little lower this time for approx. 10 seconds.

7. Hold the position, relax completely and then kick down once more. This time with 50% power, for 7 seconds.
8. Relax and repeat the reach, for 20 seconds.
9. Finally, from a relaxed stretching position once more, kick down with your full power for 10 seconds. Pushing all of your effort into engaging the leg muscles. This one will be hard work, but it also yields the best results.
10. Finally, relax the muscles and give one last reach down to your toes for 30 seconds. You should find that suddenly you can get significantly closer. The stretch has worked!
11. Don't be unbalanced. Repeat the sequence on the other side.

This concept is the core of Isometric stretching and this powerful technique can and should be applied to any stretch where you want to achieve faster flexibility. It's hard work, there is no denying it, but it also provides such rapid results that they are worth the effort.

The 30-50-100 Rule

It can be a little confusing knowing how long to hold each Isometric Stretch and how much strength to employ, especially since some stretches are complex enough on their own. As a simple rule, remember 30, 50, 100. That is; 30% power, then 50% power and finally 100% or full power.

When you work through the specific stretches later in this book, consider how you can apply the tense-stretch-relax process to each technique.

1. Tense at 30% power for 10 seconds, stretch for 10 seconds, relax 5 seconds.
2. Tense at 50% power for 10 seconds, stretch for 10-20 seconds, relax 5 seconds.

3. Tense with full power for 10 seconds, stretch for 10-30 seconds, relax 5 seconds.

As you get more advanced, consider taking the duration of tensions up. Just remember to keep your form correct and focus on targeting the muscle in question, before you start to take the intensity up. If you find results are slow to come, you may need to focus on building the muscle strength in the area you are tensing. Weak muscles don't easily allow flexibility.

As a final caveat, Isometric stretching is quite intense and should be practiced sparsely. Consider alternate days for your stretches in this manner.

Give it a go. Take your time and work hard. I think you will be impressed with the results!

FORMS OF STRETCHING

We tend to refer to stretching as a singular activity, as though there was only one way to do it. However, there are actually four main types of stretches: Static, Ballistic, Dynamic, and Proprioceptive Neuromuscular Facilitation or PNF (sometimes called Muscle Energy or Isometric). Each holds its own benefits and limitations, making them all necessary for your martial arts or fitness training.

Mixing up a variety of stretches allows for a well-balanced

routine putting the whole body through its paces and throughout this guide, you will find a combination of techniques from different forms of stretching.

Each one addresses improving flexibility and range of motion in a different way but with so many types of stretching, it can be a little confusing trying to keep the movements straight and ensure you are executing each type appropriately. Below you will find a brief introduction to each form of stretching, the benefits, the pitfalls, and how you can best apply them to your routine.

Static Stretches

Static stretching is perhaps the most famous and traditional form of stretching and for decades, static stretching was looked upon as the gold standard or default form of flexibility training.

Static techniques are also sometimes referred to as 'Passive Stretching' although this term can be a little misleading since you are still actively involved in the stretch yourself.

If you've ever seen a school gym class pulling their legs this way and that before a run or event, this is static stretching. Or if you've seen a martial artist or athlete folding forward to touch their toes, this is also static stretching.

These kinds of stretches are somewhat of an old–school approach to flexibility, they are slow and require control but can be effective if performed with care and patience. The latest research shows Static stretching has fewer benefits than originally thought in terms of increasing flexibility for functional movement types such as sports, martial arts, or even daily living. See the article "The Surprising Discovery..." later in this guide, but it's still not without benefits.

To initiate a static stretch, you will position one or more limbs so that the attached muscles and connective tissues are stretched to their current maximum length, focus on relaxing the muscle and then hold that position for several seconds or up to a minute, to initiate the stretch.

Static stretches work by gradually extending a group of muscles just to the point of discomfort. The idea is to hold the stretch in a position that challenges you within your comfort level.

Static stretching should be gentle, low-intensity, and easy to tolerate. Due to these characteristics, static stretching is widely popular and considered safe for most anyone seeking to improve their flexibility. The flip-side is that progress can be slower than other stretches due to the low resistance. The advantage is a reduced risk of tissue damage.

The key to static stretching is slow, constant force. Each stretch is held for a certain count, typically 10 to 30 seconds. For the best results, try to keep the muscle relaxed. Gradual movements can be made towards a deepened stretch, but not to the point of pain.

Some research shows that static stretches may be most effective at improving long-term range of motion (Samson, 2012) and that static stretching may also enhance overall strength, power, speed, and even jumping ability but there, other studies indicating otherwise and there are certainly limits to when it should be performed.

While possibly a good tool for low-risk flexibility training in general, static stretching should be avoided as part of a general warm-up or immediately prior to any training or competition.

One example of a common static stretch would be if you were to press the heel of one foot against the floor and reach down to lift the toes, stretching your leg to elicit a hamstring stretch.

Static Stretching

Pros:

- Generally safe / low risk.
- Easy to perform.
- Widely proven to work.

Cons:

- Progress can be very slow.
- Should only be performed after a warm-up.
- Use prior to warm-up can lead to reduced muscle power.

BALLISTIC STRETCHES

Best known for being a quick bouncing stretch, the ballistic variety of stretch is often presented as the opposite of static and offers some crossover with dynamic stretches. Here movement is used to increase the participant's flexibility. Ballistic stretches are repetitive in nature. Example: Swinging one's arms outward is considered a ballistic stretch because it relies on momentum. This momentum moves your muscle and/or joint beyond what would be considered its current range of motion. The bouncing movement used throughout ballistic stretching makes use of something called the stretch reflex. As your range of motion is stretched or bounced, the muscle and attached tendon automatically spring away to reverse the stretch.

One of the most impressive benefits of this type of ballistic stretching is that it improves the mobility of not just your muscles, but also your tendons and connective tissue. Tendon injuries, common in nearly every sport, can be reduced by this increase in stretching and elasticity.

Note that ballistic stretching certainly has its uses but should be practiced with great care in order to avoid injury and prevent your muscles from unintentionally tightening rather than stretching. Due to this risk, ballistic stretching is rather controversial in some circuits. If you are new to ballistic stretching, you may want to consult an experienced trainer for additional guidance.

That said, when done properly, ballistic stretching can demonstrate results more quickly than the previously discussed static stretching. In fact, one study from the Journal of Sports Medicine in 2010 found that in comparing participants engaged in either static or ballistic hamstring stretches for six weeks, those in the ballistic group demonstrated greater improvements in flexibility in almost half the time. These improvements were not easily won; Ballistic stretching can be physically demanding and may be best put off until you are familiar with your existing limits. However, the potential effectiveness is one reason why ballistic stretching is popular among professional athletes.

That said, as with static stretching, ballistic stretching shows little benefit if performed immediately before an athletic performance or martial arts competition. Therefore, this type of stretching is also best reserved for your flexibility training rather than being used as a warm-up or pre-performance technique.

Ballistic Stretching:
Pros:

- Faster results than passive stretching.
- Increases blood flow.
- Works joints as well as muscle tissue.

Cons:

- Higher risk of injury if performed incorrectly.
- Needs to be performed with greater care.
- More tiring.

DYNAMIC STRETCHES

If static is the opposite of Ballistic then Dynamic is a close cousin of both. Dynamic stretching is more about actively taking the body through a full range of motion than holding a stretch but it can equally involve elements of static stretching, which we will explore later in the 'Rocking' method.

Each Dynamic stretch performed is ideally customized to the demands of the activity or sport at hand. It is wise to begin each stretch at a slower pace, to ensure proper posture before increasing the velocity of the movement. The goal is a smooth and rhythmic motion that does not overwhelm the muscle. In short, dynamic stretches occur as you move, as opposed to a stretch you would stop and hold.

There is a reason that the popularity of dynamic stretching had exploded in the last decade. This type of stretching is an obvious choice for improving flexibility and range of motion but with less risk than other styles.

Dynamic Stretching has also been proven to be one of the most effective forms of combination warm-up and stretching in most exercise scenarios. The use of body motion to increase blood flow and reduce stiffness has, in many modern studies, shown far greater results than traditional methods of static and alternative stretching. Indeed, Dynamic techniques make the tissues more readily pliable and less vulnerable to injury So unlike static or ballistic stretching, dynamic stretching is a good tool to use *before* a competition or training session. Evidence even shows Dynamic Stretches can help reduce soreness *after* your training or competition too.

Plus, studies suggest that dynamic stretching warms up your muscles not just so they can stretch, but also in such a way as to activate your power (Yamaguchi, 2005) . You'll feel stronger and your muscles will be ready to deliver those powerful strikes you've been training for.

Overall, dynamic stretching will boost your performance on many levels, which is why it has fast become a favorite among athletes and fighters alike.

The only downside of these techniques seems to be that compared to a specifically held stretch targeting one or a group of muscles, Dynamic movements tend to warm up and engage a whole area, leading to greater mobility, but perhaps slower gains in terms of specific flexibility.

For optimum results, incorporate dynamic stretching into both your pre-game warm-ups and your regular flexibility training program.

Dynamic Stretches:

Pros:

- Can also work as a warm-up.
- Gets the body ready for activity.
- One of the fastest ways to improve joint mobility.

Cons:

- Can be harder to isolate specific muscle groups.
- Requires care to perform safely.
- Requires more space.

PROPRIOCEPTIVE NEUROMUSCULAR FACILITATION (PNF)

We've already explored a little about Precision Neuromuscular stretching, under another name; Isometric Stretching. Also known as PNF, Muscle Energy Technique or Facilitated Stretching. Proprioceptive Neuromuscular Facilitation utilizes both the contraction and relaxation of a muscle to increase flexibility. These kinds of stretches stimulate a response by the nervous system that stops the muscle from contracting during a stretch.

Though a bit more complex than the other forms of stretching, PNF is perhaps most effective when it comes to extending your long-term flexibility and, especially, range of motion. This could be due in part to its roots as a therapeutic tool used in rehabilitation to help patients regain mobility. In fact, a 2013 study showed that PNF stretching was significantly more effective at increasing range of motion than our old friend static stretching (Miyahara).

Nonetheless, this is definitely one more type of stretching best left for your specific flexibility training program and usually one that involves the assistance of a partner or training buddy. It should never be used as a warm-up for other stretching, and definitely never before a martial arts performance. PNF is all about pushing yourself further, which is great for extending long-term flexibility, but not great for preventing injury immediately preceding a demanding activity.

That said, one common mistake people make when they are first trying PNF stretching is that they apply the maximum force. Because PNF is all about pushing past your normal maximum flexibility, there is a tendency to erroneously assume this means by force. PNF actually works best with a gentle stretch paired with a gentle contraction. If you can visualize your maximum stretch and contraction intensity, aim for starting gently at about 30% strength. One more caution: Be sure your muscles are well warmed before you begin. If you are still a bit fuzzy about PNF stretching, here's an example to clarify:

Example: With help from a partner, lift one leg up just to that point of resistance. Then, press downward against your helper. First, tighten and then relax the leg muscles. Finally, stretch upward again and you will likely be able to go a bit beyond the original point of resistance.

PNF/Isometric Stretching

Pros:

- Possibly the most powerful technique for actually improving static flexibility in specific areas.
- Leads to real long-term gains.
- Works specific muscles easily.

Cons:

- Requires the most work and effort.
- Can cause the most discomfort.
- Ideally requires a second person to 'spot' you for technique.

PART TWO
IMPROVING YOUR STRETCHING SUCCESS

WHEN DO I STRETCH AS PART OF MY TRAINING?

Many people get confused about when to include stretching within a training regime, especially if you are already exercising as part of a class or group effort.

Should it be before you hit the gym? After your martial arts class? Somewhere in the middle?

If you've been reading throughout this book so far, you've probably come to the correct conclusion that intense static stretching should absolutely be avoided before your training, since it actually reduces power for a time after. The rest of the stretches can be fitted around your exercises in different ways, but here is an order proven to generally offer the best results:

First, some circular rotations to prepare the joints. These are relaxed and light. Gently turn the head from side to side, up and down. Circle the arms and the wrists. Twist at the waist from side to side. Bring the knee up and rotate the leg in a relaxed wide circle, repeating the same with a straight leg. Try for five to ten rotations of each.

Second, a light whole-body warm-up for one to five minutes, depending on your time available. This should be something involving the whole body and get the blood flowing. Jogging on the spot, swapping through a few stances or throwing a few very light kicks and punches are a great idea.

Next, Dynamic Stretches. These are the ones that involve moving limbs through a full range of motion and out into a stretch. Start with low, light versions and move to higher ones with full speed as you progress. Forward, side and rear leg swings are one example of this, but try to work all your limbs in all directions that you might need for your actual martial art or discipline.

Your main workout goes next. Whether you are in a martial arts class, going for a run, hitting the gym, whatever. Put your primary workout at this point in the sequence.

As you finish your main workout and start to cool down, your body is primed for the final stage; the main stretching sequence. This is the part where you include your Isometric or Static Stretches and get the most benefits from your static flexibility. Here is where you can push your muscles further, using the tense and relax sequence we explore in the chapter about Isometric techniques.

Optional. Finish with some static (relaxed holding) stretches without any muscle tension if you choose to include them in your sequence here.

For martial artists and combat students, this order of practice warms the body up before throwing it into any intense stretching and gives you the best chance of long term success.

To summarize:

Stretching as part of your training.

1. Joint rotations (5-10 of each for 1-3 minutes).
2. Light whole-body warm-up (1-3 minutes).
3. Dynamic stretches, such as leg swings (5-10 of each, working all limbs and directions).
4. Main workout or training session here.
5. Cool down / Isometric Stretching (Tense, relax and reach sequence).
6. (Optional) Static relaxed stretching.

Time of Day Makes a Difference

If you stretch in the morning and get frustrated with the results, it's worth remembering that a lot of evidence shows muscles are far more receptive to stretching and flexibility gains later in the day. This may not come as a surprise if you wake up every morning feeling stiff, but for those people who leap out of bed and jump into exercise, take care.

As a guide, consider gentle dynamic stretches before your morning workout, if you have one and if you are desperate to work on your flexibility, add some relaxed static-hold stretches after your training, run or gym session.

Save any intense Isometric or Muscle Energy stretching for late afternoon or early evening, where the results will be better, and the body will be more responsive. However, even later in the day, don't skip the warm-up and dynamic stretches. See the previous order of stretching and organize it around your training for the best results.

HOW OFTEN SHOULD I STRETCH?

If you've been reading all the previous chapters, you may be getting excited at the prospect of rapid flexibility and feel tempted to skip the Dynamic work and throw yourself into hardcore Isometric Stretching every day in an effort to see faster results ... but hold up a moment.

The bad news is, studies show that this causes the reverse to happen and the body to take longer to adapt to the demands on the muscle fibers. In other words, going too hard too fast actually slows down your results.

If you are really unlucky it can even cause injury.

The simple truth is that the more impact the muscles undergo during stretching, the more careful and balanced you have to be with your training days. Dynamic Stretching, for example, is generally considered quite safe for every day and even twice a day training, since it is low impact and reasonably accessible to most people. Isometric stretching though is at the other end of the scale. It's the hardest one to master, with the biggest impact on the body, and as such should be performed less frequently. However, it is also the form that offers the best long term results for static flexibility.

A simple, safe approach to training should look like this:

- **Dynamic Stretches:** Safe to train up to twice a day, every day.
- **Static Stretches:** Can be performed four to five times a week.
- **Isometric Stretches:** Best performed maximum two to three times a week. (Incorporate recovery days in between, using Dynamic and gentle Static Stretches instead)

For example:

- Sunday: Warm-up, Dynamic, Light Static
- Monday: Warm-up, Dynamic, Isometric
- Tuesday: Warm-up, Dynamic, Light Static
- Wednesday: Warm-up, Dynamic, Isometric
- Thursday: Warm-up, Dynamic, Light Static
- Friday: Warm-up, Dynamic, Normal Static
- Saturday: Warm-up, Dynamic, Normal Static

Maintaining your levels.

It may take a while; for some people a couple of months, others six to nine months, but once you get to the flexibility point you want. Be it high kicks, loose hips or even the splits, you can dial back the regularity with which you train

Once you hit your goal. You can halve the number of training sessions and the number of repetitions performed. So dynamic stretches can be performed every other day, static stretches a couple of times a week and once a week you can perform a quick isometric session.

That said, if you quit stretching altogether don't expect your body to maintain the flexibility levels you have worked hard to achieve.

Keep your gains, by gentle, regular training and secure that flexibility for life.

THE MOST COMMON STRETCHING MISTAKE

We live in an incredible time of sports sciences. An age where technology and the latest research has enabled us to measure the tiniest details of an individual's performance and track every slight movement during any event.

Whereas in the old days, recommendations for effectiveness were often based on anecdotes and hearsay from surly old 'experts', today we have the hard facts and figures backing up the claims, and revealing some surprising truths. Experts in the fields of sports science, psychology and kinesiology are now publishing strongly documented reports that indicate much of what we take for granted when training is actually outright wrong.

For example, it was recently revealed through large scale studies of athletes at several Universities, including Harvard, that running barefoot has significant benefits over using footwear of any kind. That's right; those $200+ sneakers with air bubbles, ridges and suspension are statistically more likely to cause an injury to you than running around with your feet in the nude.

When running barefoot your foot strikes the ground in a more natural way. The toes splay correctly and the forefoot, instead of the heel, strikes the ground earlier, generating a better form and typically reducing the risk of injury.

Not surprising when you consider pre-historic humans did just fine running around without expensive Nikes.

Another field of study revealing surprising results is that of flexibility training.

Most of us have been doing the same type of limbering up since school. We'd stand in a cold field, and with no warm-up, start pulling our legs left and right while a sadistic gym coach prepares to force us on a freezing 6-mile run.

It's a decades-old process ingrained into most people's minds when it comes to stretching, but it turns out however that these static stretches, the type where you stand and slowly pull a limb until you meet resistance, are not only useless in warming up the muscles but actually *reduces* the strength of that muscle's output for a short time afterward. This can be a major pitfall for athletes and fighters relying on kicking power.

A recent study carried out by the University of Nevada revealed that athletes produced less force from leg muscles after doing a series of static (traditional) stretches than if they had done no stretching at all. A number of other studies have revealed the same, showing that jumping straight into static stretches before an event can lead to up to a 30 percent decrease in muscle strength after stretching. These static stretches can even affect other limbs, reducing power and the ability of muscles to contract throughout the body for up to ten minutes after the stretch.

A "neuromuscular inhibitory response" is the culprit; effectively your body and muscles reacting negatively and resisting the static stretch. This early activation of the Myotatic reflex, before warm-up, causes inhibited movement and reduced range of motion. While you might feel more flexible initially, the actual muscular output is lessened and you've simply increased mental tolerance to the sensation.

Instead, all studies now point to Dynamic Stretching and whole-body Warm-Ups as the optimal way to prepare for activity.

Dynamic Stretching and Whole-Body Warm-Ups:

- Increases blood flow.
- Works full range of motion.
- Increases power.
- Improves flexibility

In fact, Dynamic techniques were shown in a recent CDC study to cut injury rates by around 50% compared with the alternatives.

Not Quite Down and Out

It's worth remembering that static stretches aren't completely without value. Sure they aren't going to help you immediately before an event (in fact they can make things worse!) but they do have a place after exercise to help muscles remain loose, retain neural elasticity and ensure blood flow. This too is backed by numerous studies.

But what if you want to get the most from static stretches as part of your routine without losing power? Next I'm going to reveal a technique to maximize the benefits of these stretches and gain flexibility in minutes, not hours!

THE 'ROCKING' TRICK FOR FASTER FLEXIBILITY

There are a number of different schools of thought regarding how to improve flexibility and the specific stretches involved but one of the most divisive elements among the martial arts, combat arts, and general fitness communities is whether static stretches still have value.

As you read through this book you will discover a lot of research about the negatives surrounding static stretches and how they can actually reduce power before an exercise. That's not to say they don't have value – they do, it's simply that static stretches are best performed after a good warm-up.

But if static stretches aren't ideal, what are?

Some recommend ballistic stretches, others dynamic stretches. One thing both these have in common is the element of movement. In other words taking a muscle group, a joint or limb through a range of movement to experience the stretch.

I've found these to be effective, but when I started to design a specific routine for improving overall flexibility it became clear that no single style of stretching held all the answers... but combined they just might.

Static stretches work, but only after some movement in the first place. Ballistic and dynamic stretches help get the body moving, but alone they don't achieve quite what most people are after. So what if we combined the two?

I'm going to share with you a trick that many people use to enhance their flexibility faster than traditional stretching alone. I call it the 'rocking method' and I believe it's one of the most powerful tactics for increasing flexibility in the long term.

No, it doesn't involve black t-shirts and head-banging but instead includes a number of subtle body movements, followed by a small manageable amount of static stretching to deliver the best of both worlds and provide real long-term gains to your flexibility. As always, a light warm-up is recommended before any stretching.

The rocking part, you might also call bumping or bouncing, but I hesitate to use these terms because it often conjures ideas of cranking the body beyond a healthy stretch and yanking the muscles into the realm of injury. Instead, the idea is to reach the point of resistance and feel that moment, then *very gently* rock the body part against that point of resistance for a count of ten bumps. These should be soft and subtle.

Following the rocks, the static stretch comes in, offering a held unmoving stretch for ten seconds.

This sequence is then repeated two more times, moving from ten rocks and ten seconds of holding to twenty and thirty. Each time increasing the depth and range of motion.

How it works.

Let's take a forward fold as the example since it is a common stretch many people wish to improve.

1. Assess your existing flexibility by bending forward and reaching to a point that feels as far as you can go. Make a mental note of this.

2. Relax, shake your legs and arms off and prepare for the next step. Breathe.
3. Go back into the same stretch, but this time, when you hit that point of resistance, gently rock up and down, bouncing your fingers over that point for a count of ten times.
4. After the tenth one, grab onto your ankles, or toes, or whatever you are comfortable with and hold the stretch in a static position for a mental count of ten seconds.
5. Relax once more. Breathe.
6. Go back down and repeat step 3, but this time for a count of twenty rocks up and down. You should find you are able to go a little further.
7. Repeat step 4, but now hold for twenty seconds in the static hold.
8. Relax and reset once more.
9. Another set of rocking, this time with thirty gentle bounces against the resistance point
10. Finish with a static hold for thirty seconds. You will almost certainly find that you are further down now.
11. Finally, relax and shake the arms and legs off one last time.

As you look at the stretches within this book, consider for each how you can apply a slight rocking motion to the stretch and how you can increase the effectiveness of each movement.

In summary:

1. 10 rocks/bounces across the point of resistance,
2. Hold the stretch for 10 seconds.
3. 20 rocks.
4. Hold 20 seconds.
5. 30 rocks.

6. Hold 30 seconds.

STRETCHING MISTAKE 2: NO PAIN NO GAIN

Ask any modern Physiotherapist or Sports Massage practitioner and they will tell you that one of the most common misconceptions regarding physical manipulation is the ethos of

"It has to hurt to help me"

Or

"No pain, no gain"

These old-school approaches to physical exercise were designed in their day to generate a tougher mental attitude to endurance and inspire athletes beyond their normal capacity. In this regard they were very successful and speaking to anyone of an older generation will show you the kind of fortitude required for training in the old days.

What they are unlikely to tell you are the injury rates and how many people were permanently damaged or forced to give up their aspirations of athletic greatness due to long term damage.

Martial arts, in particular, have a long and excessive history of physical torture for students, just as a means to demonstrate resilience. This is not to say traditional training methods have no value, simply that with modern understanding we can now see the benefits of proper alignment and body positioning.

The old ethos of pain for the sake of pain in fitness is thankfully, slowly being replaced by intelligent approaches to training that, while still exhausting and often difficult, are not catalysts for injury and long-term damage as they would have been thirty, fifty or even a hundred years ago.

Pushing yourself beyond the pain barrier is fine when it comes to cases of endurance but in stretching terms, knowing your own limits is crucial to sustaining a healthy lifestyle and avoiding injury.

This isn't to say every exercise that has been around longer than 10 years has no value. Indeed Push-ups are still regarded by most to be one of the best full-body exercises ever invented. But most modern studies show that once the body is indicating a pain response it is worthwhile listening to.

Speaking of the pain response, in the next chapter, we will explore the best way to manage your pain levels and how to ensure you push yourself while knowing the exact method to ensure you stay safe.

UNDERSTANDING THE PAIN SCALE

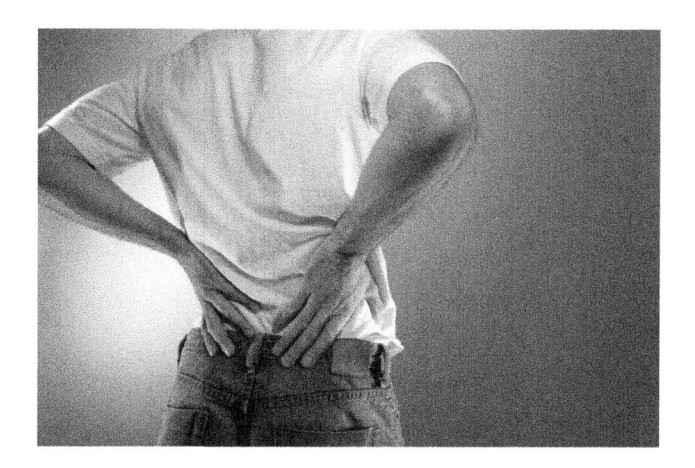

It's worth addressing the Pain Scale and understanding the difference between progress and injury early in this book because it's such an important subject, especially in regard to flexibility training.

For one reason or another, we have come to associate exercise with pain and the idea that to achieve anything worthwhile, you must push through this pain to get to some nebulous goal.

This is simply untrue. Pain does not equal success and toughness has nothing to do with it.

Do not listen to any trainer who tells you to work through any outright pain. This puts you at high risk for serious injuries, and even chronic problems in the future.

That's not to say all stretching will feel like a day at the beach. In many cases, it is appropriate to work through 'discomfort'. A small degree of this is often needed to encourage the development of greater strength and flexibility. Discomfort should be limited to fatigued muscles and soreness, primarily in the first one or two days immediately following your workout. However, immediately discontinue any activity, which causes sharp pain or stabbing or tearing sensations.

If your exercises cause pain, you may not be completing them properly or perhaps you have an old injury that is not fully recovered. It doesn't mean you are weak, or that you aren't working hard enough. Wanting to push yourself is admirable but being able to listen to your body is a more valuable skill many overlook.

By paying attention to your body, you will begin to instinctively avoid common exercise-related injuries. You can mold a routine, which is both safe and beneficial and remind yourself that staying safe and healthy is more important than speeding up your results.

Slow down and listen to your body for the sake of avoiding a long-term injury. Rest and give your body a chance to recover as needed. Use the cues your body gives you to make adjustments needed to develop a safe workout with better results.

Scoring pain the easy way.

So we know discomfort is a natural part of physical improvement. Outright pain is not. The old idea of no pain no gain is a fallacy invented by sadistic coaches to push people. This may work psychologically but the body has its limits.

But how do you know if what you are experiencing is normal and enough to 'push-through' or something that should be stopped?

The simplest method is to score your feelings on something I call the Pain Scale. An easy-to-use method for grading any pain or discomfort and knowing whether to stop or carry on.

The Pain Scale Question:

If something hurts, consider what grade out of ten you would give it? One being no discomfort at all, while ten is you heading to the emergency room.

As such, next time you stretch, give the feeling a score:

- **One to Seven – (Discomfort Level)**
- **Eight to Ten – (Outright Pain)**

Consider the below image for reference.

```
1 2 3 4 5 6 7 8 9 10
Discomfort              Pain
```

On this scale, one to seven is discomfort and common among exercise and *should* be ok. It might not feel pleasant but you should be able to push on, build muscle and improve flexibility.

Eight to ten, however, is outright pain and a signal something is wrong. Listen to your body and do not carry on if you hit this point.

Other Factors

It's perfectly normal to feel some discomfort after stretching, in much the same way you might experience stiffness or tightness the day after an intense workout or run. This is the period in which the body is rebuilding muscle tissue and getting stronger. But how else do you know if what you feel is a natural part of improvement or something telling you to stop?

We previously looked at scoring a sensation on the pain scale which is massively important, but a few other factors that can be helpful in identifying the difference between pain and normal discomfort.

1. Pain that begins immediately after you start an exercise is a problem.
2. The discomfort of muscle fatigue will usually not appear until you near the end of your set. If it shows up immediately slow down or stop.
3. Pain that limits your mobility, or appears only on one side of your body may also be a means for concern.
4. An additional factor is duration. If stiffness occurs the day after stretching, this is quite normal.
5. If pain and stiffness continues but slowly fades over two to three days, this is less ideal. It may mean you aren't quite strong enough to support the poses you are putting the body into. Specific strength training at the gym or at home, for the legs and hips, for example, can be very beneficial for this.
6. Finally, if the pain or stiffness lasts over seven days, stop and consult a doctor or medical professional.

Bottom line, always listen to your body and respect it. But, if in doubt, seek out professional medical advice. Better to make progress slow and steady, than risk injury and putting yourself out of training for a long time!

FASTER MUSCLE RECOVERY

Hot or Cold?

One of the longest-standing debates amongst Martial Artists and fitness enthusiasts, in general, has been the use of heat or ice post-event to aid in muscle recovery and injury treatment. Both have their benefits and both are frequently touted as the savior of the exhausted athlete in treating 'DOMS', aka Delayed Onset Muscle Soreness.

So which one works?

Warm-up and cool-down

Firstly, remember that warming down after exercise is just as important as warming up and yet this part is frequently overlooked. Instead of collapsing in heap on the floor or just jumping in the car to go home, try to keep the muscles active at a lower level for a short period (approx. 5-10 minutes) after they have engaged in intense exercise.

Gradually reducing intensity allows toxins to flush from the tissues and prevents the cramps sometimes associated with a sudden stop in activity. It also allows the heart and circulatory system to transition back to rest, avoiding dizziness or potential nausea.

From a flexibility viewpoint, a gradual reduction also prevents the muscles from getting tight too quickly and encourages longer-term elasticity.

- An incredibly simple approach to cooling down is to simply walk around the gym, training hall, parking lot or wherever, for a couple of minutes after intense exercise. This low-intensity movement keeps the blood flowing, helps prevent fluid 'pooling' and prevents the buildup of waste products like Lactic Acid.

First Ice, then Heat

If you have let the body cool down correctly you should reduce the chance of soreness after training, but that doesn't mean it goes away entirely. The soreness is often part of building greater muscle tissue, so it is required for growth and progression. But how can you reduce the often painful symptoms of this phase and give your tissues the best chance at quicker recovery? Do we need cold or hot to aid the body during this phase?

Both, actually.

Studies have shown that while both heat and ice are effective in treating muscles, they work in very different ways and as such should be used at different times.

Ice has the cooling effect of constricting blood vessels and reducing inflammation. Since muscle soreness is typically triggered by micro-damage to the muscle fibers, applying ice soon after an event reduces swelling and improves recovery time.

Studies have shown that athletes taking an ice bath post-exercise typically showed a 20 percent reduction in muscle soreness the next day.

If an ice bath is unrealistic (and let's face it, for most of us it is!) then a similar localized effect can be achieved through using an ice pack, or if you are really on a budget, a pack of frozen vegetables on an inflamed area.

Note: If you do choose to use ice, never apply it directly to the skin. Wrap the ice pack, frozen peas or whatever you use, in a towel or cloth first. The aim is to cool the tissue down, not freeze it, which causes long term skin damage!

Heat, on the other hand, does the opposite. Applying a heat-pack to body tissues causes the blood vessels to dilate and increased circulation to the area, which has its own benefits.

Heat is best applied much later after the initial swelling or inflammation has gone down. (Typically 24 to 48 hours + after the event).

If the muscles are still sore, but not displaying any obvious signs of damage, a heat pack applied twice-a-day for 15-20mins at a time can help increase the circulation, which in turn relaxes the area and brings increased nutrients through the blood supply. This again can speed up recovery time and reduce long-term damage.

As with ice, high-temperature heat packs should never be directly applied to the skin. Wrap these in a towel or cloth to prevent burning. Or, for an even simpler approach, have a nice hot bath. (Keep the temperature warm but not scalding.)

The next time you feel the familiar soreness after stretching or training, remember that heat and ice both have a place in your recovery routine.

1. Apply ice immediately following training, to reduce inflammation and acute discomfort.
2. Apply heat twice-a-day, the next day or up to 48 hours later, to increase blood flow and speed up tissue recovery over the long term.

WHY YOU SHOULD BE STRETCHING OPPOSING MUSCLE GROUPS

When it comes to injury prevention, we can all generally agree that one of the best things you can do is to improve the overall flexibility of your body. However, one thing we tend to forget is the value of balance. It is extremely important to strengthen and stretch both sides of each muscle. This type of approach is called stretching opposing muscle groups. The more technical term to described opposing muscles is "antagonistic." In this short chapter, let's explore why this type of antagonistic balanced stretching is so important.

If you were to measure your strength and flexibility on each portion of your body (front and back, left and right) and then compared opposite regions, you would likely come to some typical conclusions. For starters, you would see that the front of your body is probably stronger, whereas the back region is slightly more flexible. You would also likely notice that your dominant side is stronger, and the opposite more willing to stretch. This isn't really a phenomenon so much as common sense, and it isn't limited to strength training. This principle is even more important in stretching.

In our daily lives, we tend to do more lifting with our dominant side. As we repeatedly lift objects, both around the house and in the gym, those strong areas become stronger. Meanwhile, on the opposite side, there will be an equivalent lengthening—or stretching. The clearest example can be seen in the flexing of your biceps, causing a simultaneous relaxation of your triceps. Over time, this can lead to imbalance as only one muscle group is worked.

Every muscle in your body has a coordinating opposing muscle which absorbs the opposite movement. These are often referred to as flexors and extensors. Every time one group contracts, the opposing muscle relaxes. When you lengthen your hamstrings, your quadriceps contract, and vice versa.

When you consistently stretch only the front side of your body or only one portion of a muscle group, then part of that muscle becomes more flexible, while the other becomes vulnerable to over-extension related injuries. This is why it is so important to stretch opposing muscle groups.

A number of studies are also starting to show that this approach may be more effective overall. This means you'll see more improvement in your flexibility more quickly. You'll also improve the structural integrity of your body, and greatly reduce your risk of injury (Shellock, 2012).

Beyond looking better, balanced muscles feel better too. That's because imbalance can lead to strain and wear to the weaker side, eventually leading to chronic pain or acute injury. While it can be smart to isolate specific muscle groups for intense training, be sure not to neglect the opposing partner. For the best results, work every side and every angle.

Maintaining balance is as important for the beginner as it is for elite athletes. Balance isn't just about looking good; it is truly about performing better. Improved balance in the flexibility of your entire body will also improve your postural alignment, which has a large bearing on the strength and health of your spine and back. The largest benefits to working opposing muscle groups will be seen as you age (Vandervoort, 1986) in the form of fewer injuries and greater mobility compared to your peers.

Benefits of stretching opposing muscle groups:

1. Maintaining a better balance
2. Reducing your risk of injury or over-extension
3. More symmetrical appearance
4. Improved posture
5. Reduced soreness
6. Greater effectiveness in improving flexibility

Major Opposing Muscle Groups

Ideally, you should dedicate equivalent time and attention to stretching both muscles within an opposing group. The opposing groups that are easiest to identify are biceps and triceps, hamstrings and quadriceps, chest and upper back. You should also consider your abdominals and lower back as a fourth major opposing muscle group. The easiest way to reduce the lower back pain often associated with an abdominal workout is to stretch and strengthen both sides evenly, meaning the front and back and the right and left sides to avoid imbalance.

(See Part 5 for images demonstrating a number of the following techniques)

1. **Chest and Upper Back**

Simply by hunching forward and then sitting up tall, you can experience how the front chest and upper back move together, one expanding and the other simultaneously contracting. In addition to imbalanced training, additional strain is often put on the chest and back by sitting hunched over or slouched for hours at a time—as is typical for those who work at a desk or experience a lengthy commute. This can really mess with your alignment—drawing your shoulders towards your center rather than up and back—and weakening your oppositional flexibility. Stretches that engage your shoulder blades in a pulling back motion and those that encourage your chest to expand outward are a great solution towards improved posture and reduced strain.

Stretches: Seated Chest Expansion, Seated Levator Scapulae Stretch

1. **Biceps and Triceps**

Look in the mirror as you feign a bicep curl. Watch as the bicep contracts as the triceps lengthens. This is one of the clearest demonstrations of opposing muscles that tend to receive imbalanced attention. Here's a secret too many fitness enthusiasts ignore: While not as showy, your triceps are every bit as important as your biceps, especially to martial artists and fighters who need to deliver a powerful punch. Your triceps support the extension of your elbow that allows daily tasks. Both need to be able to stretch and flex to prevent hyperextension or tearing.

Stretches: Overhead Triceps Stretch, Behind-The-Back Biceps Stretch.

3. Hamstrings and Quadriceps

A simple lunge can demonstrate the importance of your hamstrings and quadriceps working simultaneously. The Glute stretches while the hamstring controls the movement. When there is an imbalance between your hamstrings and your quadriceps, the inevitable result is knee instability, potential leading to severely painful knee injuries. This may ultimately necessitate physiotherapy or even surgery in some cases. It is vital that you establish and maintain balance in the strength and flexibility of these two opposing muscle groups.

Stretches: Side-Lying Quad Stretch, Lying Hamstring Stretch

4. Lower Back and Abdominals

These two opposing muscle groups make up what is often

referred to as the core. As suggested by their nickname, they are the source of your balance and strength which is crucial for most sports. Unless they are frequently stretched and strengthened, weakness here can lead to significantly decreased balance and mobility as you age. It is not uncommon to strain the lower back when dedicating excess attention to the abdominals. It is important to work both regions equally. If you experience lower back pain, stretching these opposing muscles can lead to significant relief

Stretches: Cat/Cow Stretch and Cobra Stretch

Minor Opposing Muscles

It is worth noting the great value found in stretching minor opposing muscle groups as well. While smaller muscle regions don't get as much attention, they are equally as important to your health and comfort. This is particularly true of the extensors and flexors found on opposite sides of your wrists, ankles, and neck—coincidentally areas where people tend to experience the greatest daily strain and soreness. Use gentle stretches to work minor (but essential) opposing muscles.

Neck: Upper Trapezius Stretch, Levator Scapular Stretch.

Wrists: Wrist Extension and Flexion; Supination and Pronation.

Ankles: Achilles Stretch, Cross-Legged Ankle Stretch.

Though often undervalued, balance and symmetry continue to be important components of a well-trained body. Of all the cautions applied to stretching, this is perhaps one of the most invaluable in terms of injury prevention and flexibility improvement. Stretching opposing muscle groups won't just improve your balance and reduce your discomfort or resistance, but it actually can make it easier to plan your stretching routine by focusing on the sets of major or minor opposing groups.

WORKING WITH A PARTNER VS. GOING IT ALONE

Many times in life we work alone, be it at the gym, going for a run or simply when we are at home, but working with a training partner offers a number of great benefits, especially with stretching and flexibility work. So, which is better? Some people find more motivation and endurance while working with a partner, while others prefer to turn on some music, run solo and tune out any distractions.

Later in this guide, you will find a number of stretches dedicated to working with a partner, but it's not for everyone. This chapter takes a closer look at the benefits of partnering up or going solo so you can decide which is better for you.

Working alone is great for:

1. Focused training without distractions: For some people socializing can be empowering, but for others, it is just distracting and exhausting, especially if you are trying to focus and get in your zone. If this is you, then you'll likely prefer training alone so that you can really focus on each stretch.

2. Requires no waiting around for someone else, or working out times and meeting places: Do you like to jump into a workout or stretching regime whenever you find the time, or do you prefer to plan? If you have an unpredictable schedule, then coordinating with a partner can become a bit of a hassle. Being able to go to the gym and start working on your own terms can mean a lot more freedom, plus you won't waste time waiting for someone else to arrive. You'll also avoid the frustration of having a partner let you down by not showing up at all.

3. **Requires no holding back:** One of the biggest challenges when working with a partner is that you aren't going to be at exactly the same level. Even if you are both fit and reasonably flexible, there will always be one partner who can't move as quickly or push as hard. If you are trying to really push your own limits, it can be frustrating to have a workout buddy who can't keep up. If you work alone, then you can set your own pace.

4. **Great for clearing your head, removing the mental chatter:** A great side benefit of any training session is the opportunity to escape all the mental thoughts rolling around in your head, pushing all that away in favor of the physical challenge at hand. It can also be a good opportunity to think through personal issues. Exercise has a powerful way of clearing the mind (Bernstein, 2015). Whereas, if you were working out with a friend you might feel obligated to engage in small talk instead.

5. **You know your own body and its limits, a partner may not**: When you engage in partner stretching, you have to be extra careful to avoid injuring one another. Both the stretcher and the one aiding the stretch must be cautious about using the right positions, maintaining good balance, and not pushing too far. Otherwise, one or both partners could become injured. Sometimes it isn't physical pushing. Maybe they will unintentionally pressure you into

going beyond your body's limits. This kind of pressure can be dangerous. When you train alone, you don't have to worry about anyone's expectations except your own.

Working with a partner is great because:

1. **You tend to push yourself a little harder around others:** Studies suggest that having a workout partner can result in more repetitions being performed, especially if your new partner is supportive (Science Daily, 2016). This is partially because partnering up creates a situation in which both partners feel challenged to keep up with the other, and so both end up pushing themselves to do more. Plus, you'll feel less tempted to skip your stretching training if someone else is counting on you. Accountability is a powerful tool.

2. **A partner can stretch you in ways you simply cannot do yourself:** While you can accomplish a lot on your own, there are some exercises that can only be performed with a partner, such as those presented in the next few parts. PNF or Isometric stretches, in particular, are often easier and more effective when a partner is available to provide that external resistance. If you want a well-rounded stretching program, then you'll want to pair up to expand your options.

3. **A partner has additional bodyweight to help you:** With stretching in particular, your partner can use their bodyweight to help you leverage a better stretch. You'll be able to attain a deeper stretch, especially for techniques that move your muscle away from your own body. That means a greater range of motion without needing any extra equipment. They can also provide stability or something to hold on to. Perfect in the case of stretches like leg swings, which we will explore later.

4. **A partner can 'spot' you, reducing the chance of**

injury and correcting form: Though you may do your stretching in front of a mirror, it is still impossible to see every angle at once. A partner can provide an extra set of eyes to ensure you are maintaining proper form. This is really an invaluable benefit as just a slight problem with your posture could lead to injury, soreness, and ineffectiveness. If you are a beginner, it is highly recommended that you have an experienced partner help you attain the right forms.

5. **Training with someone else is more fun/social/motivating:** Perhaps the biggest benefit of training with a partner is simply that it is more fun. Sometimes training can feel like a solo and lonely pursuit. By training with a partner, you'll have some to talk to, making the time go faster. And, you'll be able to bounce ideas off one another to prevent the routine from getting downright boring.

Ultimately, the choice is yours when it comes to establishing a stretching practice. We can't always have a partner around, so establishing a simple solo routine should be your first priority and working with a partner should be a nice bonus; something to add to your routine as and when you can.

If you've discovered that you like the benefits explored in both categories, then don't fret. Training with a partner or training alone doesn't have to be an all or nothing pursuit. Ultimately a combination of both types of training is best for most people. You might consider training with a friend a few times each week and enjoying some more focused training alone on the remaining days. As long as you are stretching regularly, you're sure to enhance your flexibility either way.

Throughout this book, you will find a number of effective stretches you can perform alone, and a number that work best with a partner. Experiment with each to find out what works best for you.

PART THREE
WARM-UPS MADE EASY

STRETCHING VS. WARMING UP: WHY YOU NEED TO KNOW THE DIFFERENCE

When it comes to stretching versus warming up, a lot of people get confused between the two ideas. At one time, it was popular to use stretching as a warm-up, but experience and research have allowed us to improve our thinking and stop making that mistake. While there is some crossover, they are also decidedly different techniques with completely different purposes. Knowing the difference and using them appropriately could save you a lot of pain. This chapter will cover all the basics to clear any confusion you may be experiencing. Plus, it will reveal one major caution you'll want to observe.

What is Warming Up?

The purpose of warming up is to raise your body temperature and stimulate blood flow towards your muscles. In short, warming up prepares your body to do work. In this case, work can mean any type of activity including light cardio, weight lifting, stretching, or any other kind of training. Research has long confirmed that warming up before an activity will reduce the risk of musculoskeletal injury.

Though essential, warming up isn't particularly technical or complex. You just need to spend a few minutes moving your body. It can be as simple as walking around or jogging in place—anything where your body is moving. You might also include dynamic stretches or bodyweight exercises as long as they are performed correctly and are begun at a low intensity. A great idea is to simply perform the activity you are warming up for but at around 10% intensity. (More on this later).

Of course, be sure to include the part of your body that you are preparing to work. The more closely related your warm-up action is to your actual activity, the better. In Jiu-jitsu, for example, it is common to warm muscles with a series of sprawling, hip rotations, and back bridges. In other martial arts, shadow boxing, jumping jacks, or running in place are more popular.

Think of warming up as a transition between sitting still and training. A gradual curve of activity. This transition minimizes the amount of stress and sudden strain put on your body. At the same time, you will be bringing a fresh supply of blood and oxygen to the muscles. As your muscles, ligaments, and tendons warm-up, they will become more pliable and ready to work at a higher intensity.

The confusion between stretching and warming up becomes clearer when you zero in on the specific purpose—in this case literally warming up. Choose an activity that will warm your body without over-stretching, stressing, or straining. Warm your body just enough to begin to break a sweat without overexertion. Once your muscles have been warmed, they will be ready to stretch with less resistance.

What Is Stretching?

Stretching, on the other hand, is a method of straightening or extending a part of the body with the intention of increasing tissue elasticity, elongating or loosening the muscle fibers to improve flexibility. Good flexibility aids in preventing injury and extending the range of motion. When your muscles are tight, they are especially vulnerable to injury. They also leave nearby muscles vulnerable as well. Nearby muscles tend to overcompensate for the tightness, leading to damage, soreness, and/or exhaustion.

The stretches you employ will typically either be static or dynamic with occasional use of isometric or ballistic techniques. Static stretches are held in place whereas dynamic stretches are felt through a complete range of motion. While dynamic stretches have value before an event, static stretches should *never* be used as a warm-up. This can actually lead to reduced strength, power, and balance. Either practice this type of stretching hours before your physical activity, or save it for afterward.

Bear in mind that the benefits of stretching, especially static stretching, do not appear instantaneously. It can take weeks or months to expand your flexibility. A few quick static stretches before a competition may do more harm than good, but there is infinite value in consistently training your flexibility with a long-term, well-thought-out program focused on stretching after training.

Improving your flexibility is immensely important for your agility and balance, and this is done through smart stretching. As a rule of thumb, gentle dynamic stretching can be done before another activity, but static is always better afterward.

To summarize:

- Warming Up: Stimulates circulation, increases heart rate, makes muscles more pliable.
- Stretching: Improves muscle fiber (neural) elasticity and elongates tissue for added flexibility and range of motion.

Here's Where It Gets Confusing

Stretching and warming up are different. As you learned, they each have their own purpose. Hard static stretching before you warm up or before you perform an activity will generally bring no benefit, and could actually diminish your overall performance. Whereas, warming up can be extremely beneficial before stretching or competing. However, the line dividing the two isn't always cut and dry. Here's one of the biggest sources of confusion.

Before a martial arts class, dance recital or even some football games, many people will practice leg swings, taking their straight leg up high and back down a number of times. While these are a form of dynamic stretch, they are not really designed for increasing flexibility – even if it may look that way. They are simply helping to pump blood and heat to the extremities.

In even more traditional, old school classes and fitness regimes, you may see people performing the classic Quadriceps stretch, tugging their foot back toward their Glutes, while in a standing position. If possible, avoid joining in with such an exercise until either after the class or when you are at least a bit sweaty.

Static stretches should never be used as a warm-up. But some dynamic stretches, like the leg swings, can be used to warm your muscles before more intense stretching as long as you are focused on warming the muscles and joints during this phase—not trying to overstretch the tissues by pushing them to their limits.

Why Warming Up Should Always Come First

Hundreds of studies demonstrate the benefits of warming up, but Mayo Clinic, for example, warns that stretching should never be confused with warming up (2017).

Think of your muscles as being like modeling clay. If you take a cold piece out of a brand-new package and bend it forcefully, the clay will snap into two pieces. Though not as visible or drastic, your muscles are also prone to tear when they are cold. Just like working the clay in your hands warms it and makes it more pliable, warming your muscles will make them more flexible and ready to bend without injury. When your muscle fibers are cold, they aren't prepared to be stretched or stressed, and that can cause real damage. Warm muscles are more elastic and less vulnerable to acute injury.

The bottom line is that we now know that static stretching before activity does not reduce the risk of injury and can actually do quite the opposite. This isn't to say that there aren't benefits to stretching; those are explored elsewhere in this book. However, you'll want to practice your flexibility training after you are warmed up and never before another intense activity such as martial arts training or competition.

FOOLPROOF WARM-UPS USING SAID

If the warm-ups later in this guide are a little overwhelming, or you can't choose which ones to use from the thousands listed online, there is a simpler approach.

The latest research and scientific developments may be changing our opinions about sports science but interestingly these studies have also revealed the most effective way to warm- up for almost any activity and lucky for us it's very simple;

"Do what you do."

In other words, runners should run, cyclists should cycle and martial artists should practice martial arts—though at a significantly reduced intensity.

This concept stems from a popular training principle known as SAID. which means Specific Adaptation to Imposed Demands. Essentially the SAID principle indicates that specific exercises or training methods cause the body and muscles to adapt to those methods. In other words, using SAID, the body gets better at handling the demands put upon it, and warming up for this activity should ideally replicate the kind of movements you are making as you train.

For example, a swimmer would benefit from warming up with some leg and arm movements and then quickly engage in some light swimming to prepare the body for the time in the pool.

A martial artist or MMA fighter should do a bit of jogging on the spot for sparring benefits and make a few kicks or punches. (Depending on your style).

This isn't to say cross-training has no benefits, but working in a manner akin to your end goal has been shown to yield the best results overall.

It may seem obvious and yet for years, all number of new and trendy pseudo-science approaches to warming up have been adopted in different fitness circles. Thankfully, common sense is finally getting the backup it deserves from concrete results and we are now seeing some sensible approaches to warm-up exercises.

Intensity is Key

There is a slight caveat to this approach though, in that you don't throw yourself into the activity at full strength straight away. That kind of shock to the system does no good for your body. Instead introduce the exercise at a lower intensity, then a slightly higher intensity, then the full speed, normal activity.

For example, a warm-up for runners might be;

- Two minutes walking at a quick pace - 30% of normal running speed.
- Two minutes jogging slightly faster – 50% of normal running speed.
- Finally, begin to pick up the pace and run at normal speed.

A simple warm-up for Martial Artists;

- Gentle jogging on the spot or around the gym for two minutes.
- Light shadow boxing/sparring for two minutes.
- Full normal training.

This simple approach of "Do what you do" makes it easy to warm up safely and since you already know the activity there are no complicated techniques for you to work out or potentially get wrong.

1. **Your activity at 20-30% intensity for 1-3 mins**
2. **Your activity at 40-50% intensity for 2-4 minutes**
3. **Your activity at normal full intensity**

Give it a go!

PART FOUR
DYNAMIC MOBILITY

HOW TO EXTEND THE REACH OF YOUR STRIKES AND BLOCKS

Now we have a solid understanding of the theory behind flexibility, stretching and warm-ups, it's time to get into some actual techniques, beginning with Dynamic Mobility Circles or Dynamic Stretches. These are powerful exercises designed to be performed before more intense stretches and even work as part of a warm-up, but don't be fooled. They offer a great number of benefits alone.

Joint mobility is important for any kind of fitness or sports, but it plays a key role especially in martial arts, MMA and combat arts, helping you perform at the highest level. The greater range of motion and control you can establish over your joints, the greater range of defensive and attacking strategies you will have at your disposal. (Dwelly, 2009) While striking or blocking is often considered a muscle job, your joints are major players. There is an infinite number of ways to position your arm before throwing a punch or blocking an incoming blow. However, some are more efficient and effective than others—if you can pull them off. Being able to maneuver your joints into the optimal position can prevent you from losing up to 50% of your hitting power. Similarly, attaining ideal positioning can also stabilize your blocks to prevent injury.

The more flexibility and range of motion you develop in your joint, the better equipped you'll be when it comes time to assume that ideal angle. Your natural reach may be longer or shorter than others depending on the stretching ability of your muscles, ligaments, and tendons or even just your height. Either way, there is always room for some degree of improvement. Mobility circles are one of the most efficient exercises you can utilize to achieve that improvement.

One of the great things about this kind of exercise is that depending on the width and variation of the mobility circles you perform, you can also engage secondary muscle groups, offering benefits outside of the muscles you are specifically targeting.

For example, in shoulder or arm rotations you often also engage and stretch your chest and back muscles such as the Pectoralis group or the Rhomboids. In leg rotations, you may work the Gluteal muscles and the Iliotibial band.

Studies show the end result is an increased range of motion, increased flexibility, and reduced risk of strain or injury (Neperalsky, 2012). Some studies also suggest that gentle arm or leg circles may allow you to build muscle and recover from injuries more quickly. In addition to their benefit for martial artists, mobility circles are a great stretch for anyone who experiences shoulder knots or soreness.

The effectiveness of mobility circles lies in two principles:

1. Activating the muscles around a joint like the shoulder or hip joint allows this region to actually becomes more stabilized. This improvement extends to any exercise involving the shoulder or hips—such as delivering punches or kicks and absorbing blocks.
2. Stretching these joints regularly conditions the neurological response, leading to an increased range of motion, reduced discomfort, and reduced risk of injury.

One more perk of this particular stretch is that it simultaneously warms your muscles. So as long as you start slow and gentle, you may not need a pre-stretch warm-up. You'll also improve the neural connection between your limbs and brain. That means you'll be able to move faster, with more control, in a wider striking range.

Mobility circles are a great technique to add to your stretching routine. They are also a great stretch to use when you first wake up in the morning or before strength training in order to warm and activate your muscles by stimulating increased circulation. Best of all, arm or leg circles are super simple and can be completed anywhere, anytime, without any kind of equipment at all.

HOW TO PERFORM DYNAMIC MOBILITY CIRCLES

As you begin exploring mobility circles, be sure to engage your core muscles as well as the muscles in your limbs. Maintain good alignment of your back and chest. Keep your head upright and facing forward as you breathe through each rep.

If possible, we want to move in smooth, uninterrupted patterns. Remember that when it comes to dynamic stretching, the ideal is to perform fairly slow and carefully controlled movements initially, getting faster but maintaining control as the repetitions continue.

As always, don't push beyond what is comfortable.

Below are a couple of examples of simple, effective dynamic mobility stretches. For more mobility exercises, see Part 5, focused on specific techniques.

Arm and Shoulder circles:

1. Stand straight with your feet positioned shoulder-width apart.
2. Next, lift and extend your arms out to your sides, keeping

the elbows straight. For proper positioning, visualize your body assuming a neat "t" shape.
3. Now slowly rotate your arms forward, creating small circles. Aim for no more than 12 inches in diameter. Keep going for 10-20 seconds.
4. Rest for 10 seconds.
5. Next, try medium arm circles by extending the radius by a few inches. Continue for another 10-20 seconds.
6. Repeat again, this time making wider circle motions, as wide as you feel comfortable. Continue for 10-20 seconds.
7. Repeat steps 3-5. This time, try moving your arms in a backward direction.
8. Finally, give yourself one more challenge by circling your arms out in front of you.

Experiment with moving them inward, and then outward. How big can you get your circles to be?

This simple exercise, not only helps improve flexibility but can be used as part of a group warm-up drill if you are coaching or teaching a class. Start with the arms, working larger and larger circles, then move down to the legs, trying the same.

For a bonus challenge in coordination, try rotating one arm forwards, while rotating the other back backward.

Leg and Knee Circles:
Leg circles work in the same way but typically require a little more effort and coordination to complete. Another option is to start with the same technique, but only using a bent knee, moving to a straight leg later.

Below you will find my favorite version of leg circles, utilizing gradually increasing mobility to improve the whole leg, hip, and lower back flexibility.

1. From a relaxed standing position, take one leg back in a loose stance, while keeping the front leg bent. This is sometimes called a bow or walking stance. The front knee should remain over or slightly back from the front ankle. Try to avoid overstretching this to prevent injury.
2. Now, taking the back leg, bend the knee first and swing the knee up and out in a wide circle across your body.
3. As soon as the knee rotation reaches its end, put the foot down quickly and bring it back the opposite way, once again crossing in front of the body.
4. Once more, when the rotation is complete, drop the back foot back into position
5. Next, this time using a straight leg, swing the leg out in a wide circle in front of the body (following the motion previously performed by the knee).
6. Once the straight leg swing completes, bring it back again, across the body in a big circle.
7. Repeat this exercise ten times on each leg. Each time, the bent knee goes first – a wide circle, out and back. Then the straight leg does the same.
8. When you get to repetition 8, 9 and 10, really try to work the knee and leg as high and wide as you can. Fully stretch that hip joint.

Once you develop a habit of stretching your shoulder joints, hips, legs and muscles, you'll start to notice that you'll be able to strike and block faster, at an extended range, and more effectively due to experiencing less restriction when assuming the ideal angle. Remember, a clean, direct movement will allow maximum power.

DON'T FORGET TO WORK YOUR WRISTS AND ANKLES (WHY AND HOW)

When it comes to training, we tend to focus on the large, showy muscle groups. The ones that get all the attention in the media. If you hit the gym, you probably train your arms, legs, back, and abs. This is beneficial for sure, but what about the smaller, often forgotten zones? A great example of this is the wrists and ankles.

Your wrists and ankles are essential both in fitness, combat arts, and everyday life. Yet, too often we leave them to their own devices, training them only indirectly. The trouble with this is that it leaves you vulnerable to painful strains, and sprains. In the long term, failing to stretch and care for these joints can even lead to chronic ailments such as weakness, carpal tunnel, or arthritis.

One reason why wrist injury is so common is that wrists are overused and overburdened. Nearly everything we do requires some type of wrist movement. At work, they may constantly support your hands as you type. They support the steering wheel as you drive and support the groceries as you carry the overloaded bags. In the gym, they bear significant weight and force as we train. The strength and flexibility of your wrists are integral to being able to hit or punch, lifting weights, breaking boards, or pulling yourself up to the bar to complete that set of chin-ups.

The ankles too, take a beating under the burden of our whole body, every time we run, jump or walk.

Putting a significant strain on a cold, tight joint can be dangerous. Instead, you'll want to take the time to stretch your wrists and ankles, alleviating any tension, and preventing injury as you move throughout your day. Remember, more flexibility and increased range of motions means less tendency to tear or strain.

Reasons to Stretch Your Joins:

- They are used constantly.
- They bear significant force and weight.
- To improve flexibility and range of motion
- To prevent chronic (arthritis) or acute injury (breaks, sprains, strains)
- To relieve general pain or stiffness

ANKLE MOBILITY EXERCISES

While there may not be quite as many stretches available for the ankle, due to a reduced range of motion compared to the wrist, they are still an important area to work.

Standing Rotations

1. Stand in a relaxed position with feet shoulder-width apart.
2. Lift your right leg and foot off the floor to about knee height
3. Circle your ankle completely five times clockwise
4. Repeat the motion counter-clockwise five times
5. Perform the same motion on the left foot.

Seated Passive Rotations

1. Sit on a normal chair with your back upright and legs bent in a relaxed position.
2. Take your right leg and bring your right ankle up to rest

across your left knee. (Imagine the way you might read a newspaper in a cross-legged stance)
3. With the right leg supported and elevated across the left knee, take a hold of your right foot with your hands.
4. Rotate the foot through a full circle of motion five times clockwise and then counter-clockwise.
5. Repeat the process on the other foot, crossing it across the opposite knee.
6. Remember to keep the foot and ankle relaxed. This is a passive stretch, where the hands are doing the work to move the foot.

Resistance Pull

Similar to stair dips, this exercise can also stretch the lower leg muscles, foot, and ankle.

1. Seated on the floor, put both legs out straight in front, toes pointing to the ceiling.
2. Take a resistance band or, if like most people you don't have one handy, use a rolled-up towel long enough to reach around your foot.
3. Wrap the towel around your right foot and grip the ends tightly with your hands.
4. Now, using your body weight, lean back and pull with the towel, easing the toes back toward your chest.
5. Hold this position for ten seconds
6. At the end of ten seconds, push with your foot and try to point your toes straight ahead while keeping the resistance up from your band or towel. This will engage all the muscles you have just been stretching. Do this for another five seconds
7. Finally, relax the foot once more and go back into the relaxed stretch you first performed for a final ten seconds.

The isometric technique in the middle should now mean you can stretch and move a little more.

8. Repeat the exercise on the other leg.

Stair Dips

This exercise is also effective for stretching the lower leg muscles of the calf, including the Gastrocnemius and Soleus, when done correctly.

1. Find a staircase with a good-sized first step (approximately one foot in height) and a handrail for stabilizing.
2. Stand on the first step, facing forwards as if you were about to climb the steps and hold on to the handrail with one hand or both.
3. Shuffle your feet back until only the ball of the foot remains on the step and the rest of the foot (ankle and arch) are hanging in the air.
4. Now, lower your bodyweight down below the step a few inches, keeping the ball of the foot fixed and hands on the rail.
5. Keep the motion gradual and lower your weight until you feel a stretch. This may be in the top of the foot and ankle area or through the back of the lower leg.
6. Hold the low position for four seconds and then lift yourself back up to a flat-footed position.
7. Repeat the exercise ten times, with slow purposeful movements, each time feeling the stretch.

Note that this is a powerful stretch putting your whole body weight through your ankles and foot, so take care. For an additional challenge and stretch, perform the same exercise but with one foot at a time. Keeping the other slightly elevated. This will push the entire stretch through one leg, foot, and ankle.

While we often ignore the smaller muscles and joints of our body, they can be important in preserving health and improving overall performance, especially in sports or martial arts where grappling and wrist motions are involved. By taking a few minutes out of the day to perform these simple stretches, you'll safeguard your ankles and wrists and improve your performance by increasing your range of motion and increasing the amount of training your wrists can tolerate. Plus, long term your body will thank you with reduced pain or strain.

WRIST MOBILITY EXERCISES

There are dozens if not hundreds of ways to stretch your wrists. Each will target various angles or regions. Choose 2-3 good well-rounded wrist stretches to incorporate in your daily stretching routine. Here are a handful of my favorites. The key is maintaining smooth, controlled movements without overstretching or overextending. While stretching these joints is important, avoiding injury is just as much so. Always move gently with the following exercises.

Prayer Stretch

1. Stand with your palms together, as if to pray.
2. Raise your arms until your hands are directly in front of your face.
3. Move your elbows downward until they touch each other (or as near as possible).
4. Next, gradually spread your elbows apart while lowering your hands down towards your waist, stopping when you begin to feel the stretch.

5. Try to keep the palms touching as the elbows hit 90 degrees.
6. Hold this position for a count of 10 before repeating. Aim for 5-6 repetitions.

Clenched Fist Stretch

1. Sit on the floor or in a chair with your hands placed on your thighs.
2. Position your palms upward.
3. Gently squeeze your hands into fists.
4. Lift your fists up towards your body by bending at the wrist until you feel the stretch.
5. Hold the stretch for ten seconds.
6. Slowly lower your fists back towards your thighs.
7. Complete 8-10 repetitions.

Figure Eight Wrist Stretch

1. Hold your hands out in front of your body with your fingers interlaced.
2. Maintain your elbows tucked in toward the sides of your body while moving your hands around in a wide figure-eight pattern.
3. As you move your wrists should rotate, one on top at first and then the other.
4. Continue forming figure eights for ten seconds.
5. Take a short rest before repeating the stretch 3-4 times.

Eagle Wrist Stretch

This technique is often practiced in yoga and may be spotted as part of a whole-body routine.

1. Hold both of your arms out in front of you. Position them so they are parallel to your floor.
2. Next, slightly lift your right arm so you are able to cross it over your left arm.
3. Simultaneously bend both of your arms at the elbows.
4. Your right elbow should now rest in the bend of your left elbow, with the backside of each hand touching the other.
5. Twist your right arm towards the right. Twist your left arm toward the left until the little finger contact the thumb of your right hand.
6. Now press your palms together, lifting upward from the elbows while stretching your fingers upward without lifting at the shoulders.
7. Hold this stretch for 10 seconds before releasing.
8. Repeat the stretch, this time positioning the left arm on top of the right.

Fist to Stop Signal Stretch

1. Standing upright, raise one arm to shoulder height.
2. Form a fist with your hand.
3. One-by-one, open your fingers up and out so they form a "stop" signal.
4. Lower your fingers back into a fist.
5. Complete ten full repetitions.

PART FIVE
THE STRETCHES

STARTING THE STRETCHES

So now we get into all the actual stretches, the part you've been waiting for.

But hold up just a second, if you've skipped here before reading any of the other chapters, slow down a second. If you want to have a look at the stretches on offer, that's fine, but if you've jumped here and intend to dive into any of these movements without understanding the importance of the previous chapters, especially those centered around Dynamic Mobility Circles and Warm-Ups, then please take a minute to go back and review these.

Preparing for stretching is just as important as the exercises themselves and throwing yourself into exercise without proper preparation is not just less effective, it can be dangerous. Save yourself time and injuries and don't rush.

All done? Good, let's move on.

The exercises and stretches presented here are split between the stretch type and body areas. For our purposes, the upper body region is defined as the neck, arms, shoulders, and torso. The lower body region refers to the hips, thighs, calves, ankles, and feet. You will find a variety of stretches for each target group.

You will find that the stretches don't go into too much detail about the technical names of muscle groups or the anatomical terms for the body parts being used. This is again in the spirit of the Pareto principle. In other words, by keeping things simple, you are far more likely to achieve success than getting bogged down in jargon. (Still, if you are keen to learn more specifics, look out for the upcoming video course accompanying this book).

The order of the stretches in this guide is also no coincidence. They run from warm-ups to joint rotations, dynamic techniques in the order they should be practiced and only after running through all the others should you be attempting the most intense versions of static or isometric stretches.

That doesn't mean it all has to take hours. In fact, an abridged ten-minute version is perfectly fine, just ensure you go through the whole sequence first.

As a note, the only part of this sequence which can move a little are joint rotations. These can be practiced before or after the warm-up. This is a personal preference.

Remember to be patient as it may take months before you reach your goals, but you will get there through dedicated practice. Go slow until you are sure you have found the proper form to avoid injury. As mentioned in the chapter exploring the pain scale, you should stop or slow down once your discomfort reaches an eight out of ten.

(Note: Most of the images in the guide are taken from my upcoming video course. Keep an eye out for more soon.)

WARM-UPS

The following warm-ups are a small selection of some of my favorites and ones I use in the classes I teach, but the world really is your oyster. Any activity or exercise can work as a great warm-up. (See the chapter entitled 'Foolproof Warm-ups' for more.

The trick with warm-ups is to keep the intensity fairly low and try to engage the whole body to stimulate blood flow and mobility. Feel free to include these in your routine, mix up the order or include some of your own.

* * *

Sequence 1: Light
   1. Jogging on the spot – 30 seconds
   One of the simplest exercises to complete but also one of the most effective for warming up. Jogging gets the whole body engaged and encourages blood flow. If you have space you can jog around a gym or training area, but if not you can equally just jog on the spot for the same results. Try 30 seconds to start.

2. Jogging knees up – 30 seconds

Using the same principle as normal jogging, either on the spot or around a route, simply pick the knees up higher as you jog, aiming to get the thighs parallel to the ground with each movement. One option is to hold the palms out in front and make contact with each step, to ensure the legs come up fully.

3. Jogging heels back – 30 seconds

Using the same principles of jogging but this time, engaging the opposite direction, kick the heels back as you jog, aiming to gently connect with the back of the thighs or lower glutes with each movement. Again, consider dropping the palms back for something to connect with each time.

4. Cross overs – 10 repetitions

Starting with one leg forward and the other back, quickly jump up and swap the legs over, keeping that long gap between them. Then get into a rhythm of swapping the legs over, bouncing on the spot into a cross over motion. For bonus points keep the arms up in a guard type position.

5. Jumping jacks off the spot – 10 repetitions

Some people define jumping jacks and star-jumps as the same thing, but for our purpose of maintaining a gentle warm-up, we keep them separate and stay on our feet. To complete a full jumping jack, start with the feet together and arms by your side. Then quickly hop the feet out and bring the hands high overhead before returning to the start position. Get into a rhythm and complete ten.

***

Sequence 2: Intermediate

1. Mini Jumps on spot – 30 seconds

Much like using a jump-rope, without the rope, the idea of mini jumps is to use your feet and lower legs to make small micro jumps on the spot and get into a bouncing rhythm, then maintain this for thirty seconds. If you do have a jump rope, consider using this for more of a challenge.

2. Tuck jumps on the spot – 10 repetitions

Taking the previous exercise further, tuck jumps involve using that bouncing motion but now taking the legs up as high as possible into a tucked position before dropping them back down. The aim here is to be on the ground for as little time as possible.

3. Bouncing in place, arms up – 30 seconds

Now we start getting closer to martial arts techniques by maintaining that bouncing rhythm, but now introducing a guard and a fighting stance. Put one leg forward, bring the arms up into a guard and simply bounce gently on the spot. After five or six bounces, swap legs, and alternate sides, keeping the guard up at all times.

4. Throwing a jab – 10 jabs each side

Maintain that fighting stance from the last exercise, keep bouncing, but now throw out a light jab or 1-2 punch, every five or six bounces. After you throw the punch, change legs and change sides.

Keep bouncing and maintain the rhythm, being mindful to keep the punches light and relaxed.

5. Throwing a kick – 10 kicks each side

The final exercise is the same as the one above but swaps the punches for kicks. You can choose any kick you want or alternate through a few, but front-kicks and side-kicks tend to work best. Keep relaxed and light on your feet, then every five or six bounces throw your kick, keeping it fairly low and light. Change sides and repeat on the other leg, maintaining the rhythm.

JOINT ROTATIONS

Joint rotations are very simple exercises designed to put a joint through the full range of motion in a gentle effective manner. Each of these exercises should be easily performed by anyone of any ability and don't require much time to perform. Consider each one for five to ten seconds. The whole sequence shouldn't take more than a few minutes.

* * *

UPPER BODY

NECK

1. Looking Left & Right

- Begin upright, or relaxed in a chair.
- Gently move your head toward the right, as far as it will comfortably go.

- Hold this for about three seconds before moving your head all the way to the left.
- Hold here for another three seconds before returning to start to complete one rep.
- Complete five on each side in total.

2. Neck Flex and Extension

- Start out standing or sitting in a natural posture.
- Gradually drop your chin down in the direction of your chest. Hold this stretch for about three seconds.
- Come back to start and extend your neck backward, looking up to the point of resistance.
- Stay in this position for three seconds before coming back up to starting position.
- Repeat up and down three times.

3. Neck Tilt

- Start with the head upright, eyes forward
- Tilt the head, taking your ear toward one shoulder and hold for 5 seconds
- Slowly bring your head back up to the center
- Repeat on the other side
- Repeat three times on each side.

- For an additional stretch, you can gently rest your hand on your head, giving a bit more pressure at the point of flex.

* * *

ARMS & SHOULDERS

The arm and shoulder region is an area that accumulates a lot of tension in everyday life let alone through martial arts or fitness training. The stretches here are perfect for improving muscle condition and those training in styles that heavily emphasize punching and arm techniques, like Wing Chun and Boxing.

SHOULDERS
1. Shrug circles

- Start either standing or sitting upright in a chair.
- Take the shoulders up toward your ears and around in a high, slow circle back to start.
- Repeat the circle five times.
- Change direction and repeat five circles the other way.

* * *

ARMS

1. Arms Circles

- Ensure you have enough space and begin from an upright position

- Keeping the arms relaxed and long, gently swing them through the full range of motion making a high circle.
- Repeat for five rotations forward.
- Change direction and repeat for five rotations backward.

2. Wrist rotations

- Can be performed seated or standing, begin by holding the hands out in front.
- Grasp the fingers together in a gentle interlocked grip.
- With the hands moving as one, take the wrists in a full, slow figure of eight.
- Repeat three times.
- Change direction and repeat another three in reverse.

*　*　*

HIPS
1. Hips circles

- From a standing position, place your hands on your hips.
- Slowly and gently make a wide circle with your hips, going as far forward, side to side and as far back as feels comfortable.
- Keep making the circle for five rotations.
- Change direction and repeat another five the opposite way.

*　*　*

LEGS AND LOWER BODY

1. Ankle Rotations

- From a standing position, find a position of balance, with the standing leg slightly bent for stability and the other lifted a few inches from the floor.
- Take the raised foot slightly out in front and rotate the

ankle through a full circle, gently working the entire range of motion.
- Repeat five circles on direction, then five the other way.
- Repeat on the other foot.

2. Hands On Knees Rotations

- From a standing position, keep both legs fairly close together and bend the knees slightly.
- Lean forward and place your hands on your knees.
- Take both knees together through a wide circle, straightening and bending the legs as needed.
- Rotate through five circles slowly one way, and then five the other direction.

3. Bent Knee Leg Circles

- From standing, find your balance and take one leg off the ground bringing the knee straight out in front with the thigh parallel to the ground.
- Take the raised knee through a full wide circle of movement, out above your other leg, round in front and out to the side, before bringing back to start.
- Repeat five of these circles clockwise and then five counter-clockwise.
- Swap legs, find your balance and repeat the same on the other leg.

DYNAMIC STRETCHES

Dynamic stretches take the muscle through a full range of motion by engaging an agonist muscle and relaxing an antagonist muscle. They are also probably the most useful for martial artists or combat students since they help improve striking ability, speed and of course, dynamic flexibility.

Start slow and gentle with all of these stretches. In a set of ten, for example, 1-4 should be low, fairly slow and relaxed, 4-7, a little higher and faster, while 8-10 can be full speed at full height if you feel comfortable with it.

The great thing is that dynamic stretches are quick to do and even quicker to see results.

***

UPPER BODY

1. Trunk Side-Bend

- Stand with both feet spread to shoulder width.

- Put both arms above your head. Grab the opposite elbow with each hand.
- Now carefully tip first toward the right without bending your knees. Hold for a split-second and then tip toward the left doing the same.
- Come back into the center to complete your first rep.
- Complete five to each side in total

For an alternate similar exercise, move your body in the same way but reach out to the sky each side with the highest arm as you alternate from side to side.

2. Trunk Twist

- First, sit with both hands placed just behind your head. Your elbows should be aimed out toward each side.
- Rotate from your core first towards the right to the point of resistance, then return to the front before rotating toward the left.
- Get into a rhythm and complete five twists to each side.

As before, the body drives the movement, not the hands. The hands are simply there for position purposes.

3. Push, Push, Throw

- Lift both arms up in front of you so that they become parallel with the floor with elbows bent.
- Quickly tug both elbows towards your back two times.
- Complete a third tug while also turning your palms up to face the ceiling and stretching the arms out.
- Repeat the full exercise ten times.

4. High Left, High Right (Optional Extra)

- First, make both hands into fists or open palms.
- Then move one upward above your head and the second near the hip.
- Bring your arms backward to initiate a stretch across the chest region.
- To make one full repetition try easing them to the right twice and then to the left an additional two times.
- Perform three repetitions on the right and left to finish.

5. Reach over side to side.

- Start from the same position as the previous exercise, but take the feet out a little wider.
- Bring your hands up into a loose guard position and rock your weight over to the right.
- Bend the right leg as you move over to it.
- Simultaneously reach the left arm high over your head, feeling the stretch down the outside of your chest.
- Once you reach the maximum stretch, change and complete the same on the other side by transferring your weight to the other leg.

- Complete 5-10 reaches on either side at a quick but not rushed pace.

6. Side bends, side to side. (Optional Extra)

- From a standing position, drop the hands down to your sides.
- Reach slowly down to one side, pushing the fingers toward your knee, while keeping the body straight. (Try to avoid leaning forward or back).
- When you reach the maximum range, come back up to center and move across to the other side.
- Repeat five slow reaches on each side.

* * *

HIPS AND LOWER BACK

1. Fore and Afts

- To begin, arrange your body so that you are standing with the feet spread to shoulder width.
- Place your hands on the coordinating hips or to the sides of the head.
- Slowly tip forward and then back. Pay close attention to your body and each subtle motion. This stretch focuses on the abdominal and back regions.
- Complete 10 full motions forward and back to complete the sequence

Note: Do not tug the head forward and back. The hands are there for position purposes only, the body is doing the work.

2. Windmill

- Take the feet out about double shoulder width and lift both arms out toward their respective sides, making a star shape.
- Fold forward and diagonally down so that the fingers of your right hand come in contact with the toes of your left foot. (Or as close as you can get).
- Once you reach the maximum stretch or touch your toes come back up to center.
- Now fold down to the opposite side.

- Get into a rhythm and repeat five reaches to each side to complete

This exercise can also be done slightly quicker from side to side as a more dynamic warm-up.

***

LOWER BODY
1. Dynamic Knee-Crunch

- Begin standing so that your feet are spread by shoulder width.
- Quickly bring one of your knees up to your chest, or to the point of resistance. Then return the knee back to its initial position.

- As soon as the foot touches the ground, bring the knee back up once more.
- Repeat 5-10 times and on both sides.

2. Forward Leg Swings

- Start in a relaxed guarding stance.
- Take one leg back straight, while the other is bent in front.
- Swing the rear leg up directly ahead of you, ensuring to keep the leg straight to enhance the stretch.
- Start low and at a medium pace, as you increase the count, get a little higher and a little faster each time.
- Repeat for a 10 count on each leg to complete.

One of the staple warm-ups of martial arts, legs swings are a great dynamic exercise for loosening the legs and stretching the hamstrings.

3. Side Leg Swings

- Start in a relaxed guarding stance, keeping the feet about shoulder-width apart
- Keeping the right foot pointing forward and leg straight, swing the leg up and out to your side.
- As with all leg swings, start low and slow, increasing the speed and height as you perform each repletion.
- Complete ten on the right, then swap to ten on the left to finish.

Side legs swings work in an almost identical way to front leg swings except that these help work a different set of muscles including the Glutes and Hip Abductors and Adductors; ideal for styles using a lot of side-kicks (TaeKwonDo for example). This again is a dynamic exercise ideal for warming up the lower body and kicking muscles.

3. Rear leg swings (Optional Extra)

- Start from the same position as side leg swings, but this time either find a wall or a partner in front to stabilize yourself against.
- Bend one leg slightly before taking the other leg straight back behind you, working the Quadriceps and Hamstrings.
- Keep the leg relaxed and let it bend at the knee into a scorpion-like curl as it extends back and up.
- Repeat this exercise ten times on one leg and ten on the other, aiming to get slightly higher and faster with the eighth, ninth and tenth repetition.

4. Dynamic Leg Circles

- From a standing guard, take one leg forward and one leg back straight
- Next, quickly take the straight leg out at an angle across the bent leg, round in front and make a big circle bringing it gently back to the ground.
- Now, take the same leg through the same route but in reverse, finishing by coming over the other leg before resting on the ground.

- Complete five of these full circles (out and back) on each leg, changing sides halfway.

* * *

PARTNER VARIATIONS:

Having someone to work with can help you out a lot with dynamic stretches, often enabling you to focus on the stretch and use them to assist with balance and stability. Consider these partner variations if you have someone on hand.

1. Assisted Forward Leg Swings

- Start facing your partner about an arm's distance away.
- Take half a step to your right, while your partner does the same.
- Take the right leg (the outside leg) back straight, while keeping the front leg bent.
- Next bring your inside arm and hand to stabilize on your partner's shoulder, while your partner does the same on your shoulder.
- Finally, use the same process as solo front leg swings to complete partner leg swings, but this time you can both

complete the exercise at the same time with the added stability of the inside hand on your partner's shoulder.

- Partner forward leg swings are a great exercise for added stability and to get a bit more height from your practice, without the concern of maintaining balance. Still, care should always be taken to preserve your partner's stability as much as your own.

2. Assisted Side Leg Swings

- One person of the pair stands side on to the other, presenting a shoulder.
- The person performing the stretches stands with both

feet about shoulder-width apart and uses both hands to hold onto the partner's shoulder.
- Next, they complete the side legs swings as they would on their own, but now with the added stability of the partner's shoulder to hold on to.
- Complete ten swings to the right, ten to the left and then swap with the partner so both get to try the technique.

3. Horse Stance Circles

- Partner one adopts a relaxed Horse Stance (also known as Sitting Stance in some styles) by bending the legs, with both feet pointing forward and keeping the back straight.
- They then make a single punch and hold it out front.

- Partner two uses the punch as a guide to perform leg circles over.
- Using the same motion as the solo leg swings, the kicker takes the rear straight leg in a wide high circle over the punch and then back, to the start position.
- Complete five full circles there and back on each leg, before swapping roles with the partner.

STATIC AND ISOMETRIC STRETCHES

Ideally performed at the end of a routine, when the body is fully warm and prepared to stretch, static stretches and particularly isometric stretches are the ones that will help you get that deeper reach and longer flexibility from a stationary position.

Note that almost all of the static stretches in this guide can be adapted to be isometric by simply tensing the muscle being stretched for 5-10 seconds, relaxing deeper into the stretch for 10 seconds and then tensing again for another 5-10, repeating the tense-relax sequence about three times.

Remember that isometric stretches are quite intense and as such should be ideally practiced with rest days in between. Static stretches, however, are generally safer and can be practiced almost every day, though one or two days a week off can aid muscle recovery.

* * *

UPPER BODY

. . .

CHEST
1. Chest Openers

- From a seated or standing position, take both hands behind you.
- Grip one forearm in the other, much like folding your arms behind the back.
- Using arm and shoulder strength pull the arms down and slightly away from the body.
- Hold for 15 seconds.
- Feel the stretch across your chest.
- Relax and repeat three times in total.

2. Swimmers Stretch

- Start this stretch in an upright position, with feet spread to about shoulder width.
- Put your hands behind your back and intertwined as though you were holding your own hands.
- Extend the arms out so that they are fairly straight, but not so far that the elbows lock.

- Keeping the arms like this, lift them up and backward as far as you can comfortably reach.
- Now bend from your waist, moving both arms even further back. Hold this pose for about 15 seconds before relaxing back into your initial stance.
- Repeat the sequence three more times to complete.

* * *

PARTNER VARIATIONS
1. Assisted Chest opener

- One partner sits on the floor while another stands behind.
- The seated partner takes both hands up behind the head and interlocks the fingers.
- The standing partner positions so their knees are gently resting against the other person's shoulder blades.
- The standing partner then reaches forward, takes their hands down and eases the seated partner's arms gently back to the point of resistance, listening for the partner's comfort levels.
- At reaching the stretch point, hold for five seconds and relax.

- Repeat three times to complete.

ISOMETRIC VARIATION

- Complete the partner exercise as above, but this time the seated partner engages all their muscles in attempting to bring the elbows together in front of the head.
- The standing partner offers firm resistance, preventing the arms from coming together.
- Repeat this with the seated partner using 30% muscle strength for ten seconds, relax, 50% muscle strength for ten seconds, relax and then 100% for ten seconds to finish.

* * *

SHOULDERS

1. Wall stretch

- Stand perpendicular to a wall or flat surface with one shoulder close to touching.
- Reach back behind you and take your hand out, resting it

against the wall flat, arm fully extended at about shoulder height.
- Now gently turn away from the wall to initiate the stretch.
- Hold at the point of resistance for roughly five seconds before repeating two more times.
- Then repeat on the other arm.

2. Chicken Wings

- Start in either standing or in a seated position.
- Bring your right hand up and over your shoulder, reaching down to the center of your back.
- Now take your left hand underneath and behind, to meet the right hand.
- If you are able, try clasping your hands or fingers in the middle. If not, just perform the stretch to a comfortable point.
- Hold for ten seconds, relax and repeat three to four times total.
- Swap arms and repeat on the other side.

3. Cross-Body Stretch (Optional extra)

- Take one hand out in front and keep the arm straight.
- Next, take that arm straight across the chest at shoulder height out to the opposite side.
- Using your other hand, generate a gentle stretch by applying pressure to ease the stretching arm further across the chest.
- Keep the stretched arm locked out at all times.
- Hold for five seconds at the point of resistance, relax and repeat twice each side.

* * *

BACK
1. Cat/Cow

- Start on all fours with the knees under the hips and hands elbows and shoulders in line, to aid in stability.
- Take the head and chin gently up toward the ceiling at the same time as arching your back down.

- Tip the shoulders head and tailbone up while bending the middle of the back to a point of stretch
- Take a long deep breath, inhaling as you perform this full technique.
- Once you hit the maximum arch, gently and slowly breathe out as you tip the head, neck, shoulders, and tailbone down, while arching the center of the back up – performing the exact opposite as the previous pose.
- Repeat four to five times up and down, with the inhalation and exhalation each time.

2. Cobra

- Start lying on your belly, face down on the floor, body fully extended.
- Take your hands down and place them flat, next to where your shoulders would be.
- Gently and slowly, use your arms to lift your upper torso off the ground, keeping the elbows pointing back.
- Bring the head up and look forward, continuing the upward motion, but focus on keeping your hips and legs on the ground. (If they start to lift, ease back a little).
- Once you reach the full height or a height you feel comfortable with, hold for ten seconds and gently lower yourself back down.
- Repeat five to six times, breathing throughout.

3. Lying Twist

- Start lying flat on the floor, both hands by your side with one knee bent.
- Gently reach up and using the opposite hand, hold the knee.
- Next, use that hand to ease the knee sideways, across the body toward the ground.
- Keep the shoulders flat to maintain a good stretch.
- Once you touch the ground with the knee, or you feel the full range of motion, hold for five to ten seconds and relax.
- Repeat four times on each side to complete.

Optional: Double Lying Twist

- Complete the same exercise as previously described, but this time bend both legs at the knee while lying back.
- Next, keeping the knees together, twist them both slowly toward your right side, holding for three seconds.
- Keep the hands and shoulders flat on the floor.
- Gently bring the knees back to center and then down to the other side.
- Repeat four times on each side to complete.

Optional: Forward Samurai Stretch

- For this stretch, also known as Child's Pose in yoga, you may need a soft surface to work on.
- Sit down on your knees, being sure to keep your feet touching, and toes aimed backward, but open the knees wide to allow the body space.
- Tip your body down while simultaneously moving your hands along the floor as far out ahead as you can reach.

- Rest your head on the floor between your arms, relaxing each shoulder. Hold this stretch for a 15 count before carefully coming back up.
- Repeat as needed.

* * *

ARMS
1. Simple Tricep Stretch

- Start standing or seated.
- Reach up and over, position the palm of your right hand so that it rests against your back just a bit lower than your neck. The elbow should be aimed upward.
- Using the other hand, apply gentle pressure to the elbow of the arm being stretched, easing it further down the back.
- Gradually press until you reach the point of resistance. Stay in this stretch for a count of 15, relax, repeat three times total, before switching to the other side.

2. Forearm Flexion / Extension

- Start standing or sitting, with space in front of you.
- Extend one arm fully ahead and point the fingers to the ceiling as if you were to stop traffic.
- Using the other hand, gently apply pressure to bring the stretched fingers and palm back toward you, feeling the stretch in the forearm.
- Hold for five seconds, relax and repeat three more times.
- Swap to the other arm and complete.

- For the alternate variation, to work both forearm flexors and extensors, perform the same stretch but instead of pointing the fingers to the ceiling, start by pointing them to the floor.

3. Seated bicep stretch / Backbend

- To find your position for this stretch, sit on the floor.
- Now straighten your legs and place the palms of your hands down behind you so that the fingers are pointed outward.
- Gently tip the upper body backward, allowing your hands to follow until you reach the point of resistance.
- Hold this pose for about 10 seconds before returning back to start.
- Repeat three to four times to complete.

Go slowly with this motion as the back can be a sensitive area.

* * *

HIPS AND WAIST

1. Deep Lunge

- Start from standing or on all fours and slowly and gently, step forward as far as is comfortable into a long lunging position with one leg.
- Keep the front leg bent, but the knee no further forward than the ankle, to avoid pressure on the knee.
- With the back leg behind you, now extend the toes so the top (lace-part) of your foot rests on the ground.
- Your body can be either leaning over the bent leg with hands on the floor or upright, hands on the bent knee—which offers a slightly more intense stretch. (Ensure not to bend the knee beyond the foot)
- Feel the full stretch as you hold for ten seconds, then shuffle the rear leg back an inch or two and repeat.
- Hold for ten seconds, shuffle the rear leg back and repeat the sequence three times on each leg to complete.

ISOMETRIC VARIATION

As an excellent way to work toward the splits, an isometric lunge variation can be used to really engage the hip flexors and open up the whole region. Complete the exercise above as is detailed, but instead of simply holding the stretch, for every ten seconds, kick down with your rear leg into the floor/mat. You should instantly feel it in the hips.

Kick with 30% power, 50% power and then 100% power for each set of ten seconds. Ensure to relax between each for five to ten seconds, and to do both sides equally.

2. Pigeon

- Start by adopting a similar deep lunge as the previous exercise, but this time ensure you lean forward and place both hands on the floor, either side of the front foot.
- Next, shuffle the front foot sideways across to the opposite hand and allow the knee to collapse down in front of you.
- Ideally, the lower leg should be straight across in front of you forming a square shape, but if like many people this isn't possible, allow the foot to drift back a little toward your chest.
- Feel the stretch through the hips, keep the body upright and hold for ten seconds.
- To extend the stretch, lean forward and drop your chest onto the forward shin and leg.
- Drop into the stretch for ten to thirty seconds, repeating three times.
- Repeat on the other leg.

*　*　*

LEGS AND LOWER BODY

Anterior (Forward Leg) Flexibility
1. Basic Quadriceps Stretch

- Choose a spot near a wall or chair in case you need additional stability.
- Stand in a relaxed, but wide stance. Flex the left knee before raising the right foot behind. you. Move your arms so that you are able to grab and hold the right foot with either one or both hands.
- Tug gently to initiate a stretch. Hold for 10 seconds before carefully releasing the leg.
- Repeat three times on both legs.

Isometric Variation:

Complete the same exercise, but by 'kicking' into the holding hand for ten seconds each time, at 30, 50 and 100% power.

2. Bending Toe Raise

- Stand with one foot ahead of the other by around one shoulder-width.
- Lift the toes of the extended leg toward your body.
- Ensure that both legs stay straight, and tilt your whole body forward either reaching for the extended toes or stabilizing your hands on your knee.
- Feel the stretch and hold for fifteen seconds, before changing sides.
- Repeat twice more on each side.

3. Glute/Hamstring Stretch

- Start on the floor, lying on your back.
- Bend both legs, keeping the feet flat on the floor.
- Next, take one leg up and bend it at the knee, bringing the knee in toward your chest.
- Reach with your hands and grip behind the knee, gently pulling the leg tighter into your chest.

- Hold at the point of resistance for ten seconds, relax and repeat two more times.
- Repeat on the other leg to finish.

Figure Four Variation:

- Start from the same position, but this time take the one leg up and make a figure four shape, resting the lower leg/foot area against the resting knee. (As if you were cross-legged, reading a newspaper).
- Next reach behind the resting leg and grip behind the knee
- Bring the resting leg and knee toward your chest. You should feel the stretch in the bent leg through the Glutes.
- Hold for ten seconds, repeat twice more and repeat on the other leg.

4. Runners Stretch

- Start from a standing position, facing a flat wall.
- Take both hands up to stabilize yourself against the wall and take both legs back.
- Bend one leg-the front, while fully locking out the rear.
- You should feel the stretch down the back of the straight leg. If not, take it back a little further.
- Once you meet the point of resistance, hold the stretch for ten seconds, relax and repeat twice more.
- Repeat on the other leg.

Rocking Variation:

Complete the same exercise as above, but once you reach the point of resistance, gently rock your weight back and forth a few inches, feeling the stretch through the straight leg. Rock for ten seconds to complete one set. Finish with two more sets and repeat the full sequence on the other leg.

5. Dynamic-Static Calf Stretch

- Start on all fours, then take yourself up into a push-up type position.
- Raise your backside slightly into the air and then lift one leg and place that foot gently on top of the ankle of the single supporting leg.
- You should feel the stretch in the straight leg.
- Next, rock gently back and forth at the point of resistance. If you don't feel it yet, take your backside a little higher, creating a triangle shape with the ground.
- Rock for three sets of ten seconds and swap legs to do the other side the same.

6. Forward Fold

- Begin from a seated position, feet straight out in front.
- Keeping your body upright, take a deep breath and bend at the waist (not the upper back), reaching forward.
- Aim to grasp hold of your feet, but if that is not possible, start with the ankles, shins or even knees.
- Once you feel the stretch at the back of your legs, hold the position for ten seconds. Keep breathing.
- Relax back up to seated, then reach down once more, aiming to get a little lower this time.
- Hold each stretch for ten seconds, four times in total.
- The ultimate aim is to bend flat, head to knees and hands around feet.
- This stretch can also be done from a standing position, bending forward and down in the same manner.

* * *

PARTNER VARIATIONS

. . .

1. Assisted Forward Fold

If you have someone to help you out, the seated forward fold can be completed with a bit of assistance to aid with the movement. Position your partner behind you and as you reach forward and stretch each time, have them apply a little pressure to your lower/mid back to help you forward. Complete four times as before, getting a little lower and deeper each time.

Ensure your partner is gentle with the pressure and they don't push from your upper back, to avoid affecting the spine.

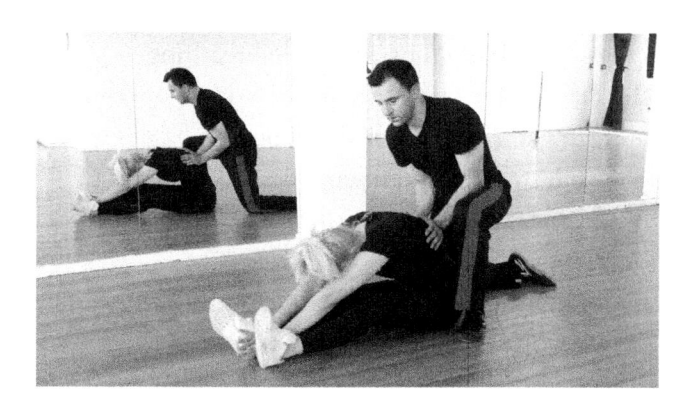

2. One-Legged Partner Stretch

- Start on your back and take one leg up straight with the sole of the foot toward the ceiling.
- Your partner steps into a deep lunge and places your heel or lower leg of the raised leg into the curve of their shoulder.
- They place their hands around your knee, keeping it locked out.
- Then as if performing a slow body tackle, they ease their body weight forward, giving you a stretch through the straight raised leg.

- Once you reach the point of resistance, tell them, and hold for about ten seconds.
- Relax a few inches, then go back into the stretch two more times.
- Complete the same three repetitions on both legs, then let your partner have a go.

Isometric Variation:

For added power and results, complete the same stretch as above, but instead of simply holding the stretch for ten seconds, kick your leg back against your partner's shoulder for three repetitions of ten seconds, with a gap/rest between each of about five seconds. First, with about 30% effort, next 50% and finally full power.

Remember Isometric stretches are more intense, so communicate and go slow.

* * *

Lateral (Side) Leg Flexibility
1. Dynamic-Static Side to Side - AKA Cherry Picker

- Start standing, and take both legs out so your feet are

about double or triple shoulder width, toes pointing forward.
- Place your hands on your hips.
- Next, slowly bend one leg at the knee and rock your weight out to that side, as you straighten the other leg.
- Once you hit the maximum range of your flexibility, gently rock your weight back to the center and then out to the other side, bending the other knee and straightening the alternate leg.
- Get into a slow rhythm from side to side.
- After ten rocks from side to side, bend one knee and hold that position,
- Reach down to your straight leg and try to get your hands around your ankle, and head to knee. (Or as far as you can).
- Hold this for five seconds, then rock to the other side and complete.

Repeat the rock and hold, four times on each side, before gently bringing yourself back to standing.

2. Lateral Split Stretch

- Ideal after completing the previous stretch, take your legs out as far as they naturally go to the sides, with toes pointing out, forming a pyramid shape with your legs.
- Reach your hands down to the ground straight ahead and hold for ten seconds.
- Next, walk your hands out to your left leg and aim to touch the left foot. Hold as far as you get for ten seconds.
- Walk your hands across to the other side and repeat for another ten on the right.
- Complete two more times each side to complete.

Isometric Variation:

Complete the same exercise as above, but keep the hands centered on the floor, then for a ten count, engage your legs, kicking down against the floor (as if you were trying to bring them together). Complete for three sets of ten seconds, with 30% power, 50% power and 100% power, resting for a few seconds between each.

3. V-Stretch Seated

- From a seated position, take your legs out wide making a V-shape, toes pointed to the sky.
- Start by reaching to the right leg, aiming to get the head on the knee and hands around the foot, or as far as you get.
- Hold the maximum stretch for ten seconds.
- Come back to the center, then over to the left and repeat on the other leg.
- Finally, come up to the center and reach straight forward, bending at the waist for ten seconds.
- Repeat twice more in each position to complete.

4. Hurdler Stretch

- From a seated position, take one leg straight forward and tuck the other leg behind you, aiming to form a right angle or box shape with the gap between the two.
- Reach forward to the straight leg, aiming for the toes and hold your maximum range for ten seconds.
- Come back up to center and then reach out at 45 degrees across the gap between the legs.
- Repeat twice more for each position and swap legs, completing the same on the other side.

5. Butterfly stretch

- From seated, take both feet into the groin and push your soles together.
- Let the knees drop down and relax.
- Grip your hands around the toes of both feet and pull yourself tighter, aiming to get the feet closer.
- Lean forward slightly to initiate the stretch, then relax.
- In between each stretch, gently rock the knees up and down.
- Complete four to six times in total.

Isometric Variation:

Complete the exercise as above, but instead of simply leaning forward, rest your elbows against the inside of the lower legs/calf muscles. Next, for a ten count, try to pull your knees together, while you resist with the elbows. Push for three repetitions, at 30%, 50%, and 100% power, relaxing for a few seconds between each one.

*** * ***

Partner Variations

1. **Assisted V-Stretch**

Complete the V-Stretch in the same way as described previously, but this time, a partner steps behind and offers a bit more help by applying hand and/or bodyweight pressure to your low/mid back at each point of the stretch, gently pushing you forward.

Go slowly and communicate how far you want to go each time, before swapping over and letting your partner have a go.

HOW TO STRETCH THE FULL BODY (ROUTINES)

The following sequences are simplified routines that work your entire body from top to toe. One focusing on the torso and arms, the other the legs and abdomen. Try them both for an overall quick and easy way to introduce dynamic stretching.

Remember, a whole-body warm-up is still recommended, and even though these techniques can help to serve a similar purpose, nothing beats getting the blood flowing before activity.

Practiced at an average pace, each sequence should take 3-5 minutes.

Upper Body Routine.

This quick dynamic sequence takes only a few minutes and focuses on loosening the muscles and joints from the head and neck downwards through the torso and arms. Perfect if you practice an upper-body heavy art like Wing Chun Kung Fu, Boxing or a Fitness regime involving free weights. Refer to the Dynamic Stretches section for more details on each.

Begin standing in a relaxed position. Feet roughly shoulder-width apart.

1. Start slowly by rotating your neck head, left, right, up and down and then side to side.
2. Perform 5 shoulder shrugs in a circle forward and back.
3. Next, extend your arms and swing them in big circles forward 10 times and backward 10 times.
4. Swing your arms across your chest so they cross over and back out to each side 10 times. (Push, Push Throw exercise).
5. Keeping the arms up in a relaxed guard, twist your torso to the left and right, keeping the eyes forward. 5 on each side.
6. Trunk side bends and Fore and Afts. 5 of each)
7. With hands on your hips slowly make a circle with the waist 5 times in each direction.

Lower Body

The lower body sequence runs through the main joints of the hip and knees; perfect for those involved in kick-heavy styles like Taekwondo or Kickboxing or for runners and people practicing leg-intensive sports.

Working down, we start from the previous sequence, standing with hands on our hips in a relaxed position.

1. Bring the knee quickly up to the chest and shoulder, before dropping to the ground. Repeat 5 of these knee crunches on each leg.
2. Again, using the knee, now make 5 circles clockwise, 5 circles counter-clockwise. Then repeat on the other leg.
3. Taking one leg straight back and complete 10 straight leg swings to the front then repeat on the other leg.
4. Complete 10 leg swings to the side on both legs.

5. Perform a full leg circle out across the body and back, 5 times on each leg.
6. Stabilizing against a wall, or partner, make 10 rear leg swings, kicking the leg straight back high like a scorpion. Repeat on the other leg.

These two quick sequences include a number of excellent dynamic techniques that should be safe to be performed as many times as you want, but they are still just a starting point. Refer to the section later, named 'Crafting your Stretching Routine', to learn how to include these, and many more techniques in a regular training plan you not only benefit from but enjoy!

PART SIX
TAKING IT FURTHER

HOW TO MAKE STRETCHING A REGULAR HABIT

It's not surprising that the most frequently reported challenge when it comes to stretching isn't so much learning the exercises as it is training ourselves to actually do it. Despite knowing the general benefits of stretching, it tends to be the one thing a lot of athletes and fitness enthusiasts are most tempted to skip. Even when they do stretch, it isn't always sufficient or consistent enough to make a real difference. So how can you trick yourself into training regularly enough to see real improvement in your range of movement and flexibility?

It would be nice if you were all born with motivation and disciple to choose a new habit and stick with it flawlessly. Unfortunately, for most of us, it takes a lot more conscious effort to stick with the healthy choices we put in place. The key here is building a habit by programming your behavior.

While you can start stretching right away, research shows that it takes a minimum of 21-30 days to transform a new behavior into a habit. It can even take up to 60 additional days to create a habit that lasts long term.

Making the Habit

If you really want to ingrain stretching as a permanent habit, then the trick, if there is such a thing, is to focus the first three to four weeks *not* on improving your performance, but on developing the habit. Don't worry too much about perfect form or pushing yourself to breaking point, simply try and keep trying, little and often.

In a way, you'll need to condition your mind before you can condition your body. Below you will find a few tips for success in establishing your stretching habit.

By applying these good strategies now, you'll be more successful in implementing your stretching practice long-term.

1. Do It Every Day

One of the biggest things you can do is to make a commitment to stretch for at least a few minutes every day. Research shows that this regularity is the key to success.

When people begin a new training program, they tend to follow the typical 3-4 days a week strategy like gym-goers. While taking time to rest and recuperate in between intense sessions is important, this type of on/off scheduling can really backfire.

In order to make stretching a regular habit, you have to do it consistently, which means every day. This allows stretching to become an automated routine, something you do almost without thinking. In the meantime, fight the temptation to skip a day. Vary your routine according

That said, it's important not to throw yourself into the most intense forms of Isometric Stretching every day. Instead, refer to the chapter 'How Often Should I Stretch?' for a safer effective approach.

Simply put, work in an extra-light day or two rather than doing nothing on "rest" days.

2. Always Stretch at the Same Time

Research also tells us that you are far more likely to stick to a habit if you undertake it at roughly the same time every day. Think about when you brush your teeth or eat your breakfast. The same is true for improving flexibility. By choosing to stretch at the same time every day, you'll be less likely to put it off while you take care of other things.

Ideally, you'll want to choose a time before you get busy, tired, or distracted. Morning is great for this but we are typically stiffer at this time of day. Early evening is another good time to choose.

- Choose a trigger. Right before dinner, or after you walk the dog. Whatever works for you.
- Do some simple stretching and take note of the time
- Repeat the action for a week, at the same time each day

3. Write an Implementation Intention

Once you have chosen a time to practice your stretching, actually sit down and write out your intention. For example, I will stretch every day at [TIME] in [LOCATION]. Studies confirm that the simple act of writing down your intention will make you 2-3 times more likely to follow through (Sadowski, 2016). Writing it down will help you mindfully process your goal and the intended result. You should also physically schedule your stretching sessions into your calendar.

4. Build Cues

Cues are especially important when you are starting to build a new habit. These cues will train your mind to remember your commitment. The more little cues you have, the better you'll equip yourself for success. One effective idea is placing your exercise clothes or workout gear somewhere you are guaranteed to see them. You might also set an alarm on your watch or cell phone as a clear reminder to stop what you are doing and go stretch. You can also write reminders on sticky notes that are placed on your bathroom mirror, office desk, front door, or refrigerator—anywhere you are guaranteed to look at least once a day.

5. Start Slow and Steady

The old adage about the tortoise and the hare is a bit overdone, but in this case, it really is true. While wanting to dive into the deep end is commendable, you'll be more likely to stick with your stretching commitment long term if you start out slow and gentle. When you start with a quick, easy, and enjoyable routine, it will feel less like work, which means you won't be as tempted to skip a session. Otherwise, you might find that you burn out early, losing that initial ambition. Stretch your enthusiasm by starting out light.

6. Don't Measure Your Progress Until Later

While you may be excited to see those initial results, it really is important to save the progress monitoring until you are at least two weeks into your new routine. One reason is that your body will need time to adjust and adapt. But more importantly, you really want to focus more on simply completing sessions and making an effort. Every day that you stick to your consistent schedule, you are succeeding in building your habit. That's what matters most in the beginning. Just doing it. Later on, you can start to track your progress and gradually increase either the duration or intensity of your stretching.

7. Make It Enjoyable

Humans are naturally predisposed to avoid any sense of pain or discomfort. On the other hand, you will gravitate towards any activity that brings a sense of pleasure or confidence. When you are beginning to build a new habit, you want to make it as fun and rewarding as possible. This way you will look forward to doing it. Move slowly and give yourself permission to really enjoy the experience.

Other options include adding some pleasurable bonuses during or after your stretching.

- Pair your stretching with your favorite music playlist.
- Stretch just before breakfast, so you can look forward to a good meal after.
- Visualize how good it would feel to be at the flexibility level you want. Imagine being stronger, fitter and more flexible. Smile, and feel good.

8. Keep Changing it Up

If you do the same routine every day, you'll likely find yourself feeling bored. Keep switching it up slightly to keep it exciting and provide new challenges. Use different body parts in different ways to maintain consistent interest. The examples of stretching routines provided in this book are just a starting point. There is almost no limit to the ways you can stretch your body, so keep exploring and expanding. Working a variety of areas in a variety of ways will also prevent you from straining any one region or reaching an impassable plateau.

That said, try not to change the whole routine completely every day. The more options you have, the more the brain resists and the easier it becomes to skip training. Keep it simple and change one thing at a time.

9. Recruit A Friend

Another great way to stay consistent is to enlist a friend with similar goals and interests. Or, find someone who had already mastered flexibility and stretching to a point where they can become a mentor. Either way, having someone to workout with will provide extra motivation because you won't want to let them down by skipping a session. Accountability is one of the most powerful motivators for all of us.

You'll also mutually benefit from being able to encourage one another. This will also allow you to explore buddy stretches that can only be performed with a two-person team. Plus, studies are actually beginning to show additional benefits to exercising with a partner compared to exercising alone (Kanamori et al, 2016). As if that wasn't enough reason, stretching with a friend is just more fun.

10. Apply Visualization When You're Tempted to Skip

For days when you are tempted to skip your session, or are just feeling a bit unmotivated, you'll want to develop a tool called visualization. Close your eyes and see the pros and cons of your decision. Visualize what will happen if you don't stretch today. For example, you'll be letting yourself down and you'll sabotage any progress you would have made. Next, visualize the benefits of diving in. You'll likely feel better when you stretch, you'll have more pride and confidence, and you'll progress towards your goal.

To summarize, here is a list of the techniques you will use to make stretching a regular habit:

- Do it every day.
- Always stretch at the same time.
- Write an implementation intention.
- Build cues.
- Start slow and steady.
- Don't measure your progress until later.
- Make it enjoyable.
- Keep changing it up.
- Recruit a friend.
- Apply visualization when you're tempted to skip.

Finally, continue to familiarize yourself with the benefits associated with your new stretching habit. Know why you are putting in the effort. The improved flexibility, range of motion and injury prevention will benefit you for years to come and being able to kick higher and faster will make a huge difference to your training. Knowing why you are doing what you are doing will serve as motivation to continue.

CRAFTING YOUR STRETCHING ROUTINE

It can seem a little overwhelming to see all the available stretches in this guide, and even these are only a small selection of the ones available. If you spend twenty minutes online, you will easily find dozens more. So how do you pick which ones to use and more importantly how do you add them into a routine, to help your practice?

While you might be tempted to grab as many stretches as possible and try to include them all in your training, studies show that keeping things simple usually leads to improved results. As such, a smaller, easy-to-remember series of stretches are much more likely to work.

Remember, that routine is your friend in flexibility. Regular training engages the SAID principle, helping the body to adapt to the demands it experiences, and ultimately demonstrate more flexibility. By changing and switching between too many exercises, workout days and having an irregular routine, you reduce the effectiveness of your training.

Try to include a little stretching every day, even if only for 5-10 minutes, then on two or three days a week, add in a specific flexibility training session, of up to twenty minutes. These sessions are the ones to include isometric stretching or more intense practices.

So which stretches do you perform on these days?

This is a difficult question to answer because everyone's needs are different. Some people simply want to maintain a level of flexibility, while others want to get the splits. Some want the upper body when others want to work the legs. It really is up to you, which ones you choose, but as a rough guide, here is a process to use as a template. Feel free to adapt to your needs.

Create Your Routine

Take your notebook or journal and jot down each day of the week, with space underneath for your chosen stretches. Then under each day include a quick note of the stretches you aim to perform. Keep it short and simple, always include a warm-up and focus on the body areas you want to improve.

Warm-up (Every stretching session)

- Choose 3 to 4 techniques from the warm-up section and write them down.
- Each is performed for roughly 30 seconds.
- Include some gentle joint rotations of all the major limbs at the start or end.

Dynamic Stretches (Every session)

- Choose 1-2 upper body techniques and write these down.
- Choose 2-3 lower body techniques and write these down.

Static (Every other day)

- Choose 2-3 specific static stretches to work areas you want to improve.

Isometric (2 or 3 days a week)

- Choose 2-3 specific techniques from the Isometric variations. Often people wish to focus on the legs here.

Remember, the first couple of weeks of your practice are set around finding what works for you, don't be afraid to change up the specific stretches for ones you prefer, or ones you find more effective. Most importantly, try to enjoy the progress. Creating a routine you find appealing will yield much better long term results.

TEST YOUR PROGRESS WITH MEASURED KICKS

Unlike cardio or strength training, the progress of your flexibility training might not be as obvious to the naked eye. After all, progress can and often should be slow, so how do you know if what you are doing is working?

One solution is measured kicks.

Performing measured kicks or measured leg swings is one powerful strategy for flexibility training that allows you to identify progress immediately and in real-time. This technique is a little more involved but much more fun than the sit and reach test that you might recall from grade school. More importantly, it is super effective for martial artists or MMA fighters.

Measured high kicks are also a great exercise for improving the dynamic flexibility of your legs, especially your hamstrings and glutes. And research shows it is even more effective than static stretching (Young, 2004). Not only are you testing your improvement, but improving as you test!

How To Perform Measured Kicks: Step-By-Step

We talk about improving flexibility a lot but being able to measure your actual progress or indeed, understand the level you are currently at is a powerful tool. This is where measured kicks come in.

At a simple level, the basic aim of a measured kick is to assess each technique you make and then try to improve the height at which you deliver those kicks by marking each one in some manner.

How do I do it?

The most effective and perhaps straightforward way to perform measured kicks is with the assistance of a heavy freestanding kicking or punch-bag if available. However, you can alternatively use a padded wall, potentially at your nearby gym, or even just a large piece of paper or ruler attached to a sturdy wall, although these are slightly less effective.

Whatever you use, ensure it is not likely to move and stable.

It may be tempting to get help from a partner holding a focus-mitt or kick shield and while this is perfect for normal kick training, it's unfortunately not effective for measuring kick height, simply because people move their arms when holding mitts, especially as the mitt takes an impact and they get tired each time.

If you choose the paper method, you'll want to be extra careful to maintain the right distance from the wall (keep your kicks a couple of inches shy of contact) and minimize the force of your kicks to prevent injury or damage should you accidentally hit the target. If you decide to practice measured kicks regularly, you'll definitely want to invest in a bag or find a gym you can use for your flexibility training. For the following process, we will assume you have a punch bag or some other static target and that you are using a single front leg roundhouse-style kick.

Measured kicks process.

1. Perform a couple of practice kicks to identify the height where you are most comfortable. (Your normal kicking height).
2. Use a piece of chalk to mark your comfort zone and draw a line. Mark two more zones, each three inches higher than the last.
3. Stand with your feet about shoulder-width apart.
4. Complete two quick kicks aimed at your comfort/lowest. Note if the chalk has been scuffed by your kick. If so, you are on track.
5. Take a short pause to reset your stance. Remember to focus on the accuracy of your height.
6. Complete two high kicks to the next marker up.
7. Finally, repeat two high kicks to the highest mark.
8. Now try again, this time kicking each marker once.
9. Return to your starting position and repeat steps 4-8 with the alternate leg.
10. Continue alternating legs until you've completed five sets on each side.

The chalk mark, especially on a heavy bag, is particularly effective for noting whether you are making contact or not. Seeing that smudged chalk line is a clear indicator that you are kicking the target and reaching your goal.

If you consistently miss one of the markers, move it down an inch or two and try again. Remember that this exercise is designed for steady progress and not to force you to kick beyond a safe limit, so use your own judgment on pushing your ability.

Once you are comfortable with this measured kick exercise, mix up the routine.

- Change your stance or distance.
- Throw different kicks at different speeds and assess your flexibility.
- Use different colored chalk marks for different heights.

Reset your comfort zone weekly or biweekly. You can also gradually increase the number of sets as your flexibility and endurance improve. Once you have some practice, you can also try the same technique with side-kicks to improve the flexibility of your Adductor Magnus and the Sartorius muscles or throw in front-kicks to engage the Glutes and hips.

As a final caveat, avoid practicing high powerful kicks on days you have worked intense Isometric Stretching. Give your body a chance to recover after specific flexibility work.

THE 'TRICK' TO LONG-TERM FLEXIBILITY

Getting flexible is all well and good, and following any number of the exercises in this guide will get you there, but how do you maintain that suppleness year after year?

There is a distinct and proven tactic for developing truly flexible joints and limbs that last.

If you look at Olympic Gymnasts or world-class martial artists as an example you will see they all have one common element of their training; regularity.

For any fitness regime, stretching plan, martial arts training or weight loss scheme the single most important element is how often you stick to the plan. It might not sound like a 'trick' in the traditional sense but it's always surprising how many people believe intensity is more important than regularity.

The fact is that doing an insane fat-burning, bodybuilding super workout once every 2 weeks is ok. Doing an average, modest level of exercise 5 times during that same period is much better.

Intense, irregular stretching sessions or workouts every now and then are very taxing for the body but regular, lower intensity plans introduce the body to a new way of working and, in turn, allow it to change and adapt to a better more healthy lifestyle.

Your Maintenance Routine

If you have designs of being flexible for the rest of your life, it's important to remember that your body is a smart thing and it adapts to the life around it.

Earlier, it was mentioned that flexibility can fluctuate according to age or activity level. This is because your body naturally adapts to the activities it engages in most frequently. If your body is used to moving in a wide range of motion, it will maintain that ability more easily. If you follow the advice presented throughout this book, then you should experience gains in flexibility that will really bolster your martial arts, MMA or fitness performance. You'll be less vulnerable to injury, and you'll have a wider range of motion for all those kicks, blocks, and punches.

However, these improvements will never be permanent without a little work to maintain your level. Your body will also adapt itself to sitting still. Have you experienced stiff hips or hamstrings after sitting for too long? As you stand, your body seems more resistant to stretching than when you first sat down. This is a short-term example of the long-term consequences of discontinuing your stretching program.

Flexibility training requires a bit more effort up-front to train the body and the nervous system to accept these new movements. Once you are at the level you require though, you can ease off the training and dial back the intensity, moving into something called a maintenance routine.

This simple series of stretches is much lighter and a little less frequent, but just as important to maintain that suppleness you worked so hard for.

Maintenance Routine.

- **Every day – 5 mins**: Perform a light warm-up and dynamic leg stretches every day. These are quick and easily undertaken for most people. 5 mins
- **Two days a week – 10 mins**: Do some moderate static stretching. Focus on the stretches you found hardest when you started out, often the legs and hips.
- **One day a week – 15/20 minutes:** Complete the warm-up and dynamic stretches, then complete two or three specific isometric stretches at a lower intensity than when you first started out. Again, focus on the ones you found hardest, to begin.

By establishing a simple maintenance routine you can keep your flexibility levels high and enjoy all the hard work you put in to get there, without the levels of effort previously required.

CHEAT SHEET: YOUR STRETCHING SIMPLIFIED

This book contains a lot of information and I understand it can be a little overwhelming. So, to make things easier, here is a quick cheat sheet, summarizing the main topics and the most essential information to keep you safe. This isn't an excuse to skip the rest of the book, nor is it a substitute for real understanding, but providing you have already at least glanced over most of the content, this should serve as a handy summary.

Essential Information:

1. Flexibility is neurological. A response sent via your brain to your muscles telling them to contract and keep you safe. We are not stretching the muscle length, but actually the body's tolerance to these kinds of movements.
2. You are already 'flexible' enough at a muscular level to do almost anything you want. (Including the splits!)
3. Flexibility comes in three main forms. A. Dynamic – such as leg swings and kicks, B. Static – such as reaching

as far as you can and holding it. C. Active. Such as holding a high kick in the air. Dynamic is the most useful for most martial artists.
4. Understand the pain scale to avoid injury. 1-7 is discomfort. 8-10 is pain. Stop at anything over 8.

Order of Stretching:

1. Warm-ups should *always* come first. (Possibly including joint rotations).
2. Dynamic Stretches come next.
3. Your main workout or exercise would go third.
4. Finish on either Isometric or Static stretches.

Regularity:

1. Dynamic stretches can be performed every day.
2. Static Stretches on alternate days
3. Isometric Stretches should be two or three days a week (These are the most intense).

Warm-Ups:

Essential before any stretching or exercise. As an easy way to warm up, consider the SAID principle and do your activity at:

- 30% intensity.
- 50% intensity.
- Then at full normal intensity.

Joint Rotations:

Help bring fluid and mobility to joints, reducing injury and extending your joints. Simply move each joint through a slow wide circle. Refer to the section on Joint Rotations for specific techniques.

Dynamic Stretches:
Ideal for martial artists and fighters. Dynamic movements involve taking a limb through its full range of motion at increasing speed and intensity.

- Start slow and low. Approx. 20% speed, 20% height.
- In the middle move, to roughly 50% for speed and height.
- Finish at maximum speed and height.

Refer to the chapter on Dynamic Stretches for specific techniques.

Static Stretches:
Also known as reach stretches, involve stretching as far as you can and holding it while relaxing the muscle in an effort to condition the muscular response to the movement.

- Go slowly.
- Breathe during each technique.
- Try to relax the muscle at maximum stretch.
- These can be enhanced with Isometric and/or Rocking techniques.

Refer to the chapter on Static and Isometric Stretches for specific techniques.

Isometric Stretches:
Isometric Stretches are the most intense but also the most effective techniques for improving long term static flexibility. They require tensing the stretched muscle, relaxing and then moving further into the stretch. As a simple guide.

1. Tense at 30% power for ten seconds, relax the muscles and move a little deeper into the stretch.

2. Tense at 50% power for ten seconds, relax and move deeper.
3. Tense at 100% power for ten seconds and make the final stretch.

Rocking Method:

As a simple way to enhance static stretching, utilize the rocking method.

1. Find the maximum stretch point.
2. Gently rock at that point, reaching just over the stretch and back with a gentle ongoing bounce.
3. Relax, go deeper into the stretch and repeat.
4. See the section 'The Rocking Method', for specific timings and repetitions.

Maintenance Routine:

Maintenance is essential to keep your levels of flexibility after reaching the standard you are happy with. Intensity and regularity can be reduced, however.

Recommended:

- **Daily:** Warm-ups and dynamic stretches.
- **Twice weekly:** Static stretches.
- **Once weekly:** Isometric techniques.

- See the chapter 'Your Maintenance Routine' for more details and durations.

THANK YOU FOR READING

I hope you found this book interesting and the techniques help you on your road to improved flexibility and a greater range of motion, whether you are competing, training or just want to explore what your body is capable of.

Finally, if you enjoyed any of the tips and methods included, please leave a quick review.

I work hard to create useful and easy-to-follow guides for martial arts, fitness, self-defense, and well-being but I do all this on my own and I don't have a publisher's backing like many authors. If you found this book insightful, or feel like you learned something new, please take 30 seconds to leave a few words.

Positive feedback makes a world of difference to me and other readers alike so thank you for shaping the future of my books!

- Phil Pierce

READY FOR MORE FLEXIBILITY?

Ready to take your flexibility further? Discover **How to Stretch for Martial Arts, MMA and Self Defense: Your Ultimate Stretching and Warm up Guide** ... the video course!

https://geni.us/flexibility

What's inside?

- Over 80 videos, packed with proven stretches and techniques to increase flexibility.
- Step-by-step guide through safe and effective warm-ups.
- Dynamic stretches for increased range of motion and mobility.
- The exact methods for releasing muscle tension for faster, higher kicks, and longer-reaching strikes.
- Stretching 'hacks' so you can cheat your way to increased flexibility quicker than ever.
- And more!

Visit: **https://geni.us/flexibility** and unlock the potential in your flexibility today!

This publication (and any by this Author) may not be copied or reproduced in any format, by any means - electronic or otherwise - without prior consent from the copyright owner or publisher.
All content Copyright © 2020.

This guide is not associated with any Martial Arts organization.
All content herein is considered a guide only.
No liability accepted for any injury associated with the practice of Martial Arts, Self Defense or any other activity.

❊ Created with Vellum

Printed in Great Britain
by Amazon